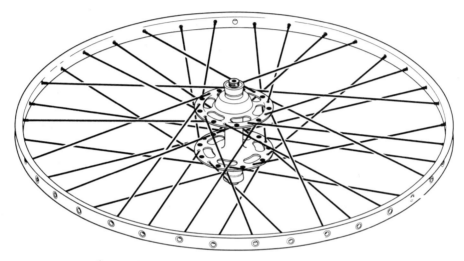

the
Bicycle Wheel

the Bicycle Wheel

Second Edition

Jobst Brandt

Illustrated by Sherry Sheffield Boulton

AVOCET, INC.   MENLO PARK

CALIFORNIA

Avocet, Inc., Menlo Park 94026

© 1981, 1983, 1988 by Avocet, Inc. All rights reserved. Reproduction of
the whole or any part of the contents in any form without written
permission from the copyright proprietor is prohibited.
Published in 1981. Second Edition 1988
Printed in the United States of America

First printing 1981
Second printing 1983
Third printing 1985
Fourth printing 1987
Fifth printing 1988
Sixth printing 1989
Seventh printing 1990
Eighth printing 1990
Ninth printing 1992

Library of Congress Catalog Card number 81-69715
ISBN 0-9607236-4-1

ACKNOWLEDGMENTS

As most projects, this one was not the product of a single person. The advice and suggestions of friends and supporters were valuable contributions. Even the comments of those who saw no merit in the project helped form the completed work so that it contains many subjects that, otherwise might not have been included.

I am especially grateful to Jim Westby for his tireless efforts to edit the engineering jargon into common English and for managing the production of the second edition. Lee Chen applied the rules of an engineering report to the work so that definitions precede usage and descriptions progress in a logical order. Joel Harrison developed the computer program that solved the wheel deflection equations, and John Adelsbach developed the curve-fitting method that was used to plot the results. The illustrations were made by Sherry Sheffield Boulton, who also designed the book.

Inspiration for many subjects came from the Hjertberg brothers of Wheelsmith. There were many critics and proofreaders, each of whom added perspective to the text. I am also grateful to those who built wheels in order to test the correctness and clarity of the wheel-building instructions.

Throughout the long development of this project, Bud Hoffacker of Avocet patiently supported my efforts and encouraged me to continue. I hope all those who contributed share my satisfaction with the quality of the finished work.

TABLE OF CONTENTS

INTRODUCTION   3

THE WHEEL: ANCIENT AND MODERN   5

PART I
THEORY OF THE SPOKED WHEEL   7

Loads   9
How the Wheel Supports a Load • 11

The Wheel Stands on its Spokes   14

Static and Dynamic Loads   17
Radial Loads • 18   Wheel Deflection • 19   Braking
Loads • 21   Lateral Loads • 24   Torsional Loads • 26

Effects of Torsional Loads · 26   Pulling and Pushing
Spokes · 26

Wheel Failure 30

Wheel Collapse · 30   Component Failure · 31   Metals
and Stress · 31   Metal Fatigue · 32   Spoke Failure · 34
Rim Failure · 35

Wheel Strength 37

Strength and Durability 38

Stiffness 39

Radial Stiffness · 39   Lateral Stiffness · 40   Torsional
Stiffness · 43   Enough Stiffness · 44

Components 47

Spokes 48

Straight Spokes · 48   Butted Spokes · 48   Elbowless
Spokes · 49   Flat and Oval Spokes · 50   Other Special
Spokes · 50   Spoke Thickness and Performance · 50
Spoke Threads · 51   Spoke Twist · 53   Spoke Materials · 53

Spoke Nipples 54

Nipple Lengths · 54   Hex Head Nipples · 54

Rims 56

Rim Design · 56   Aerodynamic Rims · 57   Rim Spoke
Holes · 57   Rim Joint · 57   Rim Materials · 58   Wood-Filled
Rims for Tubular Tires · 59   Anodised Aluminum Rims · 60
Braking Characteristics · 60   Brake Heating · 61

Hubs 62

Hub Design · 62   Small- and Large-Flange Hubs · 63
Flange Diameter and Torsional Stiffness · 64   High-Low
Rear Hubs · 65   Torsional Stiffness of the Rear Hub · 67

Wheel Design 69

Number of Spokes 70

Spoke Patterns 71
Radial Spoking • 71   Crossed Spoking • 72   Number of
Spoke Crossings • 72   Interlaced Spokes • 72   Identical and
Mirror-Image Spoking • 73   Combined Spoking Patterns • 74

Spoke Tension 76

Improving the Spoke Line 77

Stress Relieving 79
How Stress Relieving Works • 79   How to Relieve Stress • 79

Tied-and-Soldered Spokes 81

PART II
BUILDING AND REPAIRING WHEELS 83

Parts and Tools 85

How to Select Components 86
Rims • 86   Hubs • 86   Spokes • 86   Nipples • 87
Spoke Wrench • 88   Getting Ready • 89

Inserting the Spokes 90
The First Spoke • 91   All Hubs • 92   The First Set • 93
The Second Set • 94   The Third Set • 96   Crossing the
Spokes • 96   The Fourth Set • 99

All The Spokes Are In 100

Tensioning The Wheel 102
Warning • 102   Taking Out The Slack • 102   Making Them
Tight • 102   Tension by Tone • 103   Improving the
Spoke Line • 103

Truing the Wheel 106
Small and Large Errors • 106   Five-, Six-, and Seven-Speed
Wheels • 107   Radial Truing • 107   Lateral Truing • 109
Centering • 109   The Rim Joint • 111   Final Tensioning • 111
Wind-Up • 112   Finding the Right Tension • 112   Balancing
Tension • 113   Stress Relieving • 113

The Wheel is Finished 115
Tying and Soldering · 115

Other Spoke Patterns 116
Radial Spoking · 116   Key Holed Hubs · 116

Mixed Spoke Patterns 118
Spoking One Side at a Time · 118

Wheel Repair 121
Spoke Failure · 121   Soft Wheel Failure · 122   Dented
Rim · 122   Replacing a Rim · 124   Reused Spokes · 124

Optional Tools and Their Uses 125
Truing Stand · 125   Centering Tool · 125   Nipple
Driver · 127   Tensiometer · 127

**PART III
EQUATIONS AND TESTS** 129

Tying and Soldering 131

Spoke Strength 132

Equations 134
Spoke Lengths · 134   1. Spoke Length · 135   2. Torsional
Elasticity of Spoking · 136   3. Spoke Elongation from
Tension · 136   4. Torsional Stiffness of Tangential
Spoking · 136   5. Torsional Stiffness of a Typical Hub
Shaft · 137   6. Torque Transfer to Left Side of Hub · 137
7. Rim Compression from Spoke Tension · 138   8. Constricting
Force of Inflated Tire on the Wheel · 138

Finite Element Computer Analysis 139
Radial Load · 141   Braking Load · 142   Radial and Braking
Load · 143   Torque Load · 144   Radial and Torque Load · 145

Glossary 147

the Bicycle Wheel

_Introduction

In the early 1960's when I first tried to build wheels, I discovered that there was little "how to" information available. I found little about why wheels are built with different hubs, rims, spokes and spoke patterns. There were no books, and magazine articles gave little help. What advice I gathered was vague and in part contradictory.

With time and experience I discovered how to build good and durable wheels and how to avoid failures. By trial and error I learned how various components affect wheels and what usually goes wrong if a wheel is incorrectly built. I hope that this book, which is a collection of what I discovered, will help you avoid many of the pitfalls and failures that I experienced.

I have divided the subject into three parts. Part one, theory, explains how wheels respond to loads. It discusses the merits of various designs and components, and explains what causes failures. Part two, practice, gives a step-by-step guide for building front and rear wheels and wheels with different patterns and numbers of spokes. Part three, data, contains test results and formulas for computing spoke lengths and other wheel dimensions.

THE DISC WHEEL

Since the first edition of this book, disc wheels have been allowed in bicycle racing. I believe this is unfortunate because they do not improve enjoyment of the sport for the participant or the spectator. Disc wheels are expensive, heavy, dangerous in winds, and cannot be used to advantage in general cycling. This emphasis on technology diminishes the importance of athletic ability. Because they are not in general use and are not manually built, their construction is not included.

The Wheel: Ancient and Modern

Although the origin of the wheel may be obscure, its invention as a load carrying device marked the advent of machinery. Today the wheel is an essential part of most machines in the form of gears, pulleys, cams, sprockets and shafts. However, the wheel still is most visible as a load carrier and, among load carriers, the bicycle wheel stands out as one of the most refined.

The bicycle wheel with tensioned steel spokes came into use more than a century ago, replacing wooden wheels with thick rigid spokes. It was a major improvement, important to the development of the lightweight bicycle, advancing performance by increasing strength while reducing weight. Today's elegant, lightweight tensioned wheel can carry loads of more than a hundred times its own weight. Although most people are familiar with the bicycle, few understand how its wheels achieve this unusual strength.

This strength is demonstrated, for example, when a bicycle with a passenger on the handlebars is ridden off a curb without damage. The six-inch drop from a curb can give a jolt of more than three G's to cause a force of more than four times a rider's weight on the front wheel. This maneuver is especially impressive because it is usually performed on poorly maintained wheels.

Since the skills of wheel building have been handed down through apprenticeship, little record of the technical knowledge that underlies this craft can be found. Lore and mystique crept in, in the absence of a written record. Because it was so difficult for me to discover the techniques for building true and durable wheels, I felt compelled to put what I found into writing so that this information would not be lost.

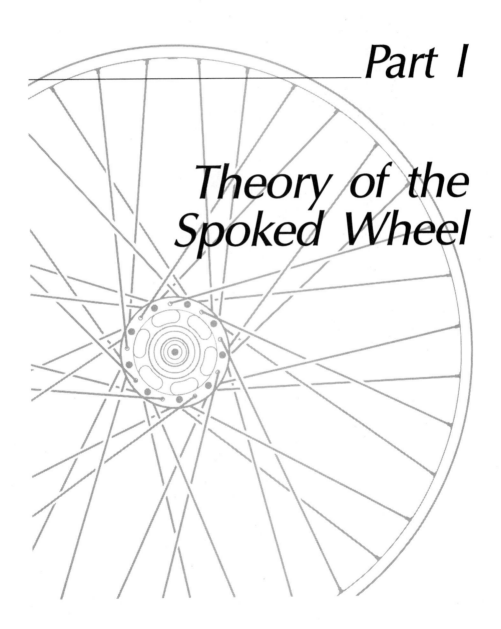

Part I

Theory of the Spoked Wheel

INTRODUCTION

The hub, rim, and spokes work together to support the bicycle in an apparently obvious way. You might suspect that the hub hangs from the upper spokes. This, however, is not true. The wheel works differently from the way it appears to work and seems to defy common sense. I will develop a number of engineering concepts to demonstrate how spokes do their work.

Let us consider only the structural parts of the wheel (hub, rim, spokes, and nipples) and the loads that affect them. The wheel is held together by spokes that are stretched between the hub and the rim. The spokes are adjusted and held tight by threaded nipples screwed onto their ends. The axle, bearings, and tires are not part of this structure.

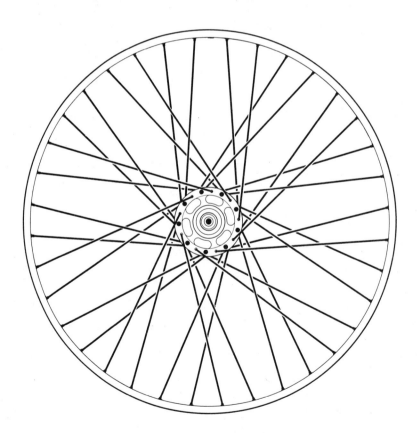

LOADS

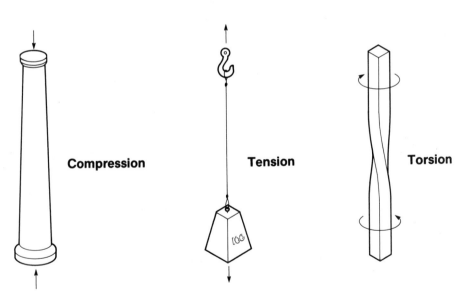

Compression **Tension** **Torsion**

Fig. 1 Compression, tension, and torsion

In the wheel there are static and dynamic loads, each of which has radial, lateral and torsional components. Static loads (such as spoke tension in a wheel at rest) do not change, or change rarely. Dynamic loads (such as the weight of the rider on the rolling wheel) change continually with use. Although the rider's weight remains unchanged, it causes changing forces in the rolling wheel. Both static and dynamic loads combine to cause stress in the wheel.

The radial, lateral and torsional loads make the wheel bend and deform. This deformation is usually invisible because, although forces may be high, deflections are generally too small to be seen. The deformation makes the parts stretch from tension (pull), shorten from compression (push), and turn from torsion (twist).

Let us look at what causes radial, lateral and torsional loads, and what they do to the wheel. Then we can see which parts of the wheel deform the most and why they break.

HOW THE WHEEL SUPPORTS A LOAD

The wire-spoked wheel is no different from a wooden spoked wheel in the way it works. A wooden wheel transmits loads from its hub to the ground by pressing on its bottom spoke. That spoke is slightly shortened as it furnishes the upward force to carry the hub. In the wire-spoked wheel the bottom spoke is also shortened, but instead of gaining in compression, it loses tension. The change in force is the same for either wheel. The spoke sees a net increase in force equal and opposite to the downward force on the hub.

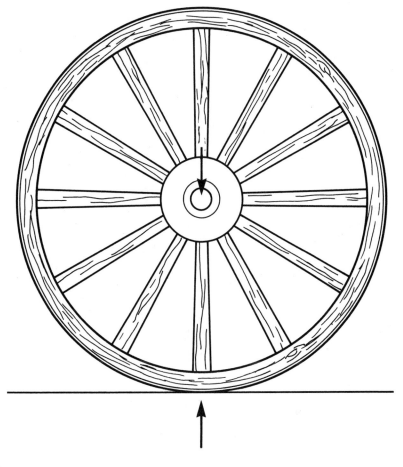

Fig. 2   Loaded wagon wheel

Because light weight is so important to the efficiency of the bicycle, heavy wooden spokes of the earliest bicycle wheels were soon replaced by pre-tensioned thin steel wires. Wires must be pre-tensioned because although they are very strong, they only support loads in tension, and a spoked wheel supports loads in compression. Pre-tensioning the wires prevents them from becoming slack when compressed.

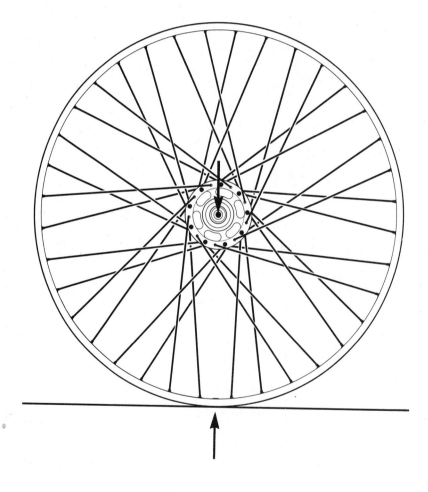

Fig. 3 Loaded bicycle wheel

A simple test can show that only a few spokes at the bottom of the wheel are affected by a vertical load. With someone sitting on your bicycle, try the following experiment to determine which spokes become tighter or looser when the wheel is loaded. The tone of a plucked spoke, just as the pitch of a guitar string, gives an indication of tension. By listening to the plucked spoke with and without load, you should be able to hear a change in tone. A higher tone indicates more tension.

To get the best tone, pluck the spoke with your fingernail near the nipple while the wheel is loaded and unloaded. Do not compare spokes to each other; instead, use the same spoke at different positions. When the spoke is at the bottom of the wheel it should make a different tone than when it is at the top. Trying this at various positions around the wheel, with and without load, will show which spokes are affected by the rider's weight. Be sure to sit on the saddle. Do not stand on one pedal or you will introduce side loads that alter the results.

THE WHEEL STANDS ON ITS SPOKES

Of course the wheel can't stand only on the bottom spokes. Without the rest of the spokes, the bottom ones could not even be tight. Standing, in this case, means that the spokes at the bottom are the ones that change stress; they are being shortened. Structurally these bottom spokes respond the same way rigid columns respond to loads. They do this only because they are pre-tensioned along with all the other spokes.

Fig. 4   Wooden wheel

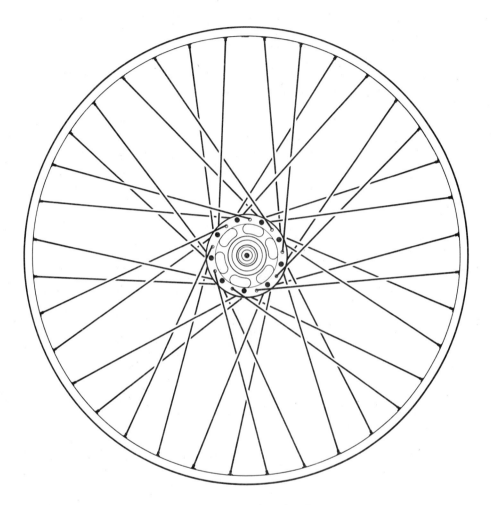

Fig. 5   Bicycle wheel

A similar condition occurs in structures that use stone or concrete in what appears to be tension. These materials cannot work in tension just as wires cannot work in compression. However, concrete is used as a tension member in many structures. A concrete bridge beam sags at mid-span under load. The sag compresses the top surface and stretches the bottom. Although the underside elongates it is not in tension. It is pre-stressed in compression by internal steel rods that ensure no part of the beam will experience tension.

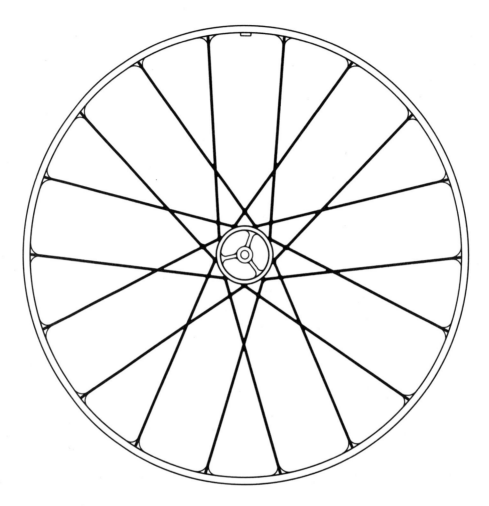

Fig. 6   Cast bicycle wheel

Because it is pre-stressed, the wheel can stand on the bottom spokes. All the action is in these spokes, not in the top ones. Structurally, bottom spokes are acting as compression members. None of the elastic movement in the wheel reveals, under any measurement, that the spokes are anything but rigid compression columns. The wheel can only be analyzed through the concept of pre-stressed wires. The idea that the hub hangs from the upper spokes contradicts the measured and computed behavior of the spokes and rim.

STATIC AND DYNAMIC LOADS

The greatest static load in the wheel is the spoke tension. The combination of all the spokes pulling inward on the rim compresses the rim with a force of about a half ton. This compression force can be computed from the number of spokes and their tension using equation #7 in Part III. Spoke tension directly effects rim compression so that as average spoke tension changes, rim compression changes proportionally.

Although spoke tension is the rim's principle static load, tire pressure also compresses it. When inflated, a tire tries to become shorter and fatter. The force with which this occurs depends on its cord angle and air pressure. A tubular racing tire, inflated to 8.5kg/cm for instance, tries to shorten with a force of 30kg. For clincher tires (used on most bicycles), air pressure pushes inward on the bed of the rim and pulls outward on the hooked rim edge. These two forces exactly cancel each other; only the effect of the cord angle causes a net inward force. Using the tire cross section and cord angle, the constriction can be computed in a similar way as for a tubular tire (see equation #8 in Part III) by accounting for the missing open part of the tire casing.

Because clincher rims without hooked sides do not capture the tire bead, pulling forces in tires mounted on them do not help reduce the inward force of air pressure on the rim. The cord angle of the tire can have no effect on these rims because the forces in the tire are supported entirely by its bead. Because tires on these rims cannot be inflated to high pressure, their change in rim compression is about the same as for high pressure clinchers.

The principal dynamic load on the wheel is the weight of the rider combined with the effect of bumps in the road. There are also radial, lateral and torsional loads caused by pedaling, braking, and riding while standing. These loads combine to bend and twist the wheel elastically. These dynamic loads are the cause of wheel deterioration and, finally, failures such as broken spokes, and cracked rims and hubs. In contrast, static loads within the wheel are essential to its structure but do not directly contribute to wheel failure. For this reason we will focus mainly on the effects of dynamic loads.

RADIAL LOADS

Radial loads distort the rim radially in the plane of the wheel. Other than the static spoke tension, they are always dynamic loads. They are called radial because they displace the rim radially in contrast to the displacement caused by lateral or torsional loads. The portion of the rim that is deformed is called the load-affected zone. Most stress changes occur there and it can be considered the working zone of the wheel.

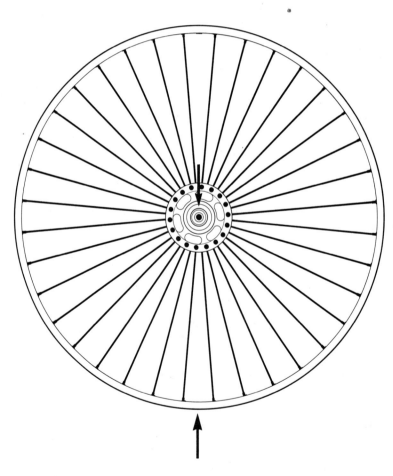

Fig. 7   Radial loads

WHEEL DEFLECTION

Using a spoke tensiometer, tension changes of a single spoke can be measured through one wheel revolution. Although the method works well enough to verify theory, it is cumbersome and not sufficiently repeatable for accurate comparisons among spokes. For analysis of wheels in general, a mathematical model was developed to compute wheel deformations using the finite element method for structural analysis.

In the computed analysis, the wheel is assumed to be two dimensional, or flat, which represents an accurate model for radial loads. The wheel diameter, rim and spoke cross sections, and the elasticity of the rim and spokes are used to describe the wheel. From these values, the rotation, and the radial and longitudinal displacement of the rim at the end of each spoke is computed. Smooth curve fits of the results are displayed on a spoked wheel diagram to show, in exaggerated deflections, how the wheel responds to various radial loads including torque and braking.

In Figure 8, rim deflection in the load affected zone is exaggerated so that slight flattening appears as a smooth dent in the rim. The illustration shows that the diameter of the rest of the rim is slightly enlarged with small bulges at the ends of the flattened area. This increase in diameter causes an insignificant increase in spoke tension of less than four percent of the change experienced by the spokes in the load-affected zone. Because the increase in diameter is uniformly distributed around the rest of wheel it causes no lift. It does not make the hub "hang from the top spokes" as is sometimes suggested. The increased diameter results from flattening the arch of the rim at the bottom.

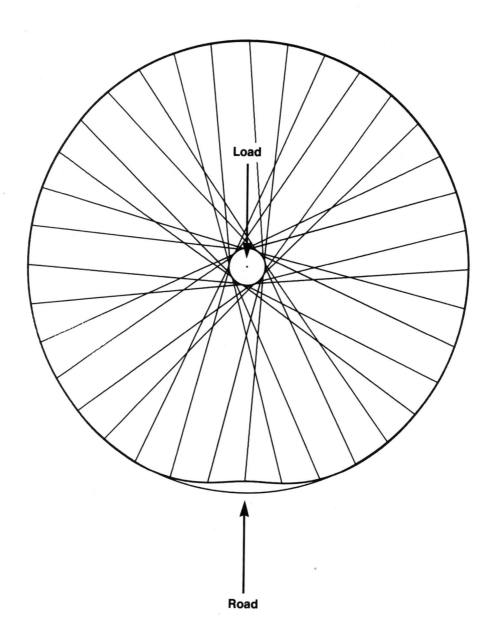

Fig. 8   Radial load

BRAKING LOADS

Braking with a caliper brake causes small but significant radial loads that affect spoke tension. Under hard braking, the brake shoes retard the rim with a force of up to 50kg by pushing rearward with 25kg force and pulling on the front half of the rim equally. This increases compression in the rear half and decreases compression in the front half about the same as the increase from tire pressure. This change in rim compression affects the spoke tension. (see Figures 9 and 10)

In a wheel with average tension, the spokes in the forward part of the wheel become about 5kg looser and the spokes in the rear, 5kg tighter. At the caliper and the ground contact point, where the forces enter the rim, there is little effect and spoke tension remains unchanged. The bending stiffness of the rim causes a smooth transition in spoke tension as the rim passes through the brake caliper. Braking causes the only significant increase in rim compression that the wheel experiences. This increase in rim compression can make an over-tensioned wheel become pretzel shaped during severe braking.

COMBINED RADIAL AND BRAKING LOADS

In figure 10, the two effects are combined as they would normally be in an actual wheel. The deflections represent the shape a front wheel would take under severe braking.

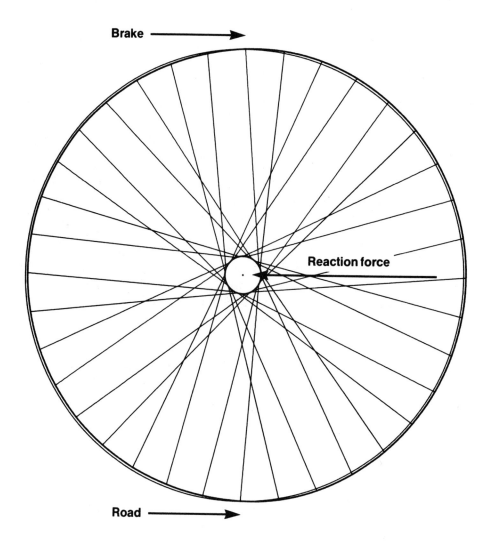

Fig. 9   Braking load

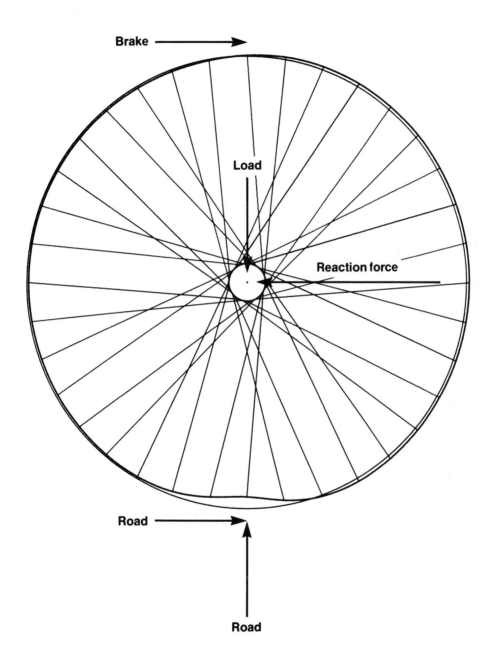

Fig. 10   Radial and braking load

LATERAL LOADS

Lateral loads, those from the side of the bicycle, act at right angles to the plane of the wheel. Because the bicycle leans in curves and is controlled by balance, its wheels need much less lateral strength than radial or torsional strength. Laterally wheels have less than one tenth their radial strength. There are no lateral loads on the wheels of a bicycle ridden in a straight line or ridden through flat or banked curves, unless the rider leans to either side.

Pedaling while standing and leaning the bicycle from side to side causes only moderate side loads. However, pedaling at high speed while seated can cause yaw and roll forces from the imbalance of the moving legs. These forces can make the wheels leave the ground and land at an angle to the direction of travel. This can cause wheel collapse. Lift-off can also happen on a bumpy road with the same result. Damaging side loads can also occur when one or both wheels slip in a turn, then suddenly regain grip. The cause of these failures is not usually recognized by the unfortunate rider.

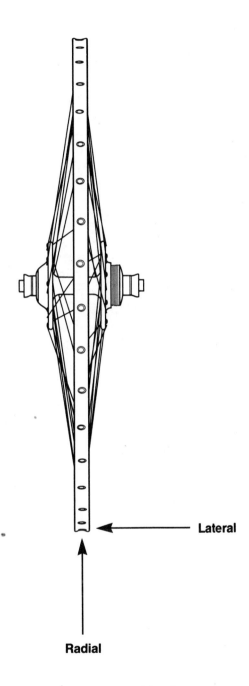

Fig. 11   Radial and lateral load

TORSIONAL LOADS

Pedaling or using a hub brake generates torque. Torque is a dynamic load that turns (or stops) the wheel. It is a twisting force such as on a screw turned by a screwdriver. On the bicycle, the chain turns the sprocket of the rear wheel and puts torque into the hub. The hub turns the wheel by changing the spoke tension so that half the spokes become tighter and half become looser. The tighter ones pull forward on the rim and the looser ones pull backward. In the pre-tensioned wheel, therefore, half the spokes pull and half the spokes push the rim to turn the wheel.

EFFECTS OF TORSIONAL LOADS

Torque, from pedaling or a hub brake, is a dynamic load. Unlike pedaling, a hub brake produces continuous uniform torque. It causes dynamic changes as the wheel turns. Torque changes the rim compressive force at the ground contact point where part of the rim pushes toward that point and part of it pulls away. This change in rim compression makes the spoke tension higher in the pushing region and lower in the pulling region. For a small-flange hub the tension change is about plus and minus 10kg for strong pedaling or braking forces, or less than half the effect that tire pressure has on spoke tension.

The effect of torque on the spokes depends on the amount of torque, the number of spokes and the flange diameter of the hub. Torque is the product of a force and a lever. The longer the lever, the more torque will result from a given force. Conversely, the longer the lever the less force will result from a given torque. In the wheel, the flange radius is the lever arm through which the torque acts on the spokes. For given torque, spoke tension change (force) becomes less as the flange (lever) becomes larger. However, even with small-flange hubs, the strongest pedaling has little effect on spoke life. The changes in tension are about one tenth of those caused by the weight of the rider on a smooth road.

PULLING AND PUSHING SPOKES

Torque, unlike other loads, affects all spokes equally but in two directions. Half the spokes become tighter and half become equally looser. All the spokes are involved, not just the pulling ones. Total torque is equal to the tension change, times the number of spokes, times the flange radius. The spokes that become tighter are pulling and the ones that become looser are pushing. The pulling spokes stretch and become longer

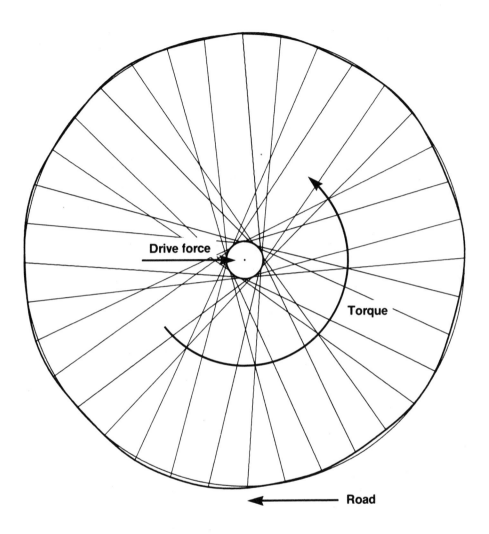

Fig. 12   Torque load

and the pushing spokes compress and become shorter. The rim bulges inward at the pulling spokes and bulges outward at the pushing spokes. The average tension in the spokes and the average rim compression remain unchanged.

Of course the pushing spokes don't push in the usual sense because they are wires and they are not in compression. In the pre-stressed wheel, however, they act as if they are pushing. In an unloaded wheel, without torque, the spokes are in equilibrium and at the same tension, but with torque pulling and pushing spokes become tighter and looser in pairs.

In the following illustrations the effect of torque is shown alone and then combined with a vertical load. Torque causes changes in tension that appear as waves in the rim. The waves in the left side of the wheel are above the average, and the ones on the right below the average. This difference arises because the road pushes to the left. The rim responds to the pulling and pushing spokes as though they were rigid columns. The pulling spokes pull the rim inward and the pushing spokes push it outward. Because they are tangent to the hub but point in opposite directions, they must pull and push to produce torque in the same direction.

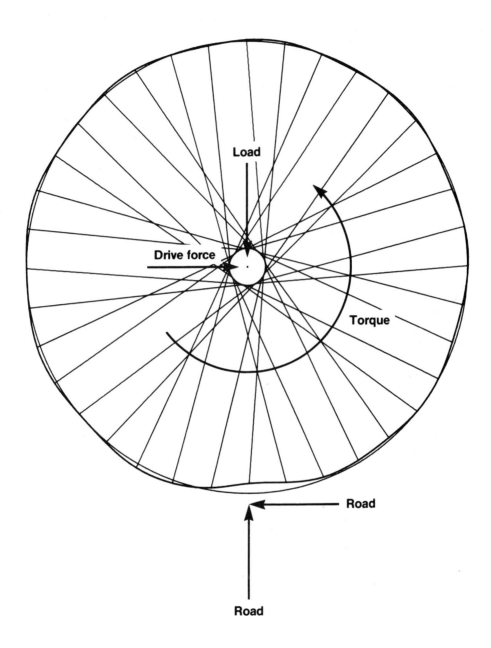

Fig. 13   Radial and torque load

WHEEL FAILURE

Most wheel failures are not dramatic. Although wheels sometimes collapse they usually fail gradually by losing alignment. In a broad sense, wheel failure means that through some defect, the wheel becomes unusable. It may become so misaligned that the tire rubs on the frame or the brakes drag. Wheel collapse is more sudden and is usually caused by a side load. Although gradual deterioration is less obvious than collapse, its effects can be detected and it can be controlled.

WHEEL COLLAPSE

Wheels collapse from several causes, but the result is usually the same. The rim is forced to one side where the tire touches the ground and the wheel becomes pretzel shaped. Another less common failure occurs when the rim breaks and releases all spoke tension. This can happen when the wheel strikes a curb or falls into a grating in the road.

Most wheels collapse during a crash or an event that causes a large lateral force. The rim is forced to one side, either as the result of a crash or the cause of it. Radial overload can contribute to wheel collapse. For instance, if a bicycle were ridden off a sufficiently high curb, the bottom spokes would become loose and leave the rim laterally unsupported. At this moment even a small side force could displace the rim enough to cause collapse.

Usually a wheel becomes too crooked to ride before its spokes are loose enough to allow collapse. However, as a wheel deteriorates, loose spokes will continue to loosen progressively faster, making the possibility of collapse from both radial and lateral loads more likely.

In the following illustration, wheel collapse is divided into stages as it takes on the common pretzel or potato chip shape. As the rim is deflected to the left at the road, the ends of the deflected section lie at an angle to the plane of the wheel. The stiffness of the rim resists the sharp bend shown in the first stage and pushes the middle of the wheel to the right, causing an ''M''-shaped wave.

The top of the wheel responds similarly to the ends of the ''M'' and moves to the left, the same as the bottom of the wheel, to complete the saddle shape. The rim stiffness and its compression cause each of the four humps of the saddle to reinforce the adjacent humps until spoke tension is lost. With small rim displacement the wheel can spring back, but with large displacements, spoke tension begins to decrease, and the rim settles into a new shape which is permanent.

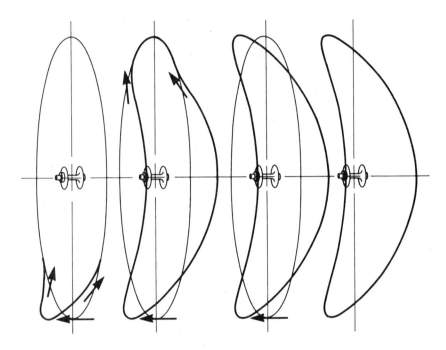

Fig. 14   Wheel collapse

COMPONENT FAILURE

The wheel components that commonly fail are the spokes and the rim. They fail both from sudden loads, as in a crash, and from fatigue. Although the effects of fatigue are invisible, they can be retarded by careful wheel building. The hub and spoke nipples are not subjected to sufficiently large dynamic loads to suffer metal fatigue.

METALS AND STRESS

Metals such as steel and aluminum are elastic materials that spring back if they are deformed or bent. If they are bent far enough they take a set, and do not return entirely to their original shape. The stress level at which a metal takes a set is called its elastic limit or yield point. Below the elastic limit the metal works in its elastic stress zone. Above the elastic limit it is forced into its plastic stress zone. Beyond the plastic zone is the failure stress at which the metal breaks. Brittle metals have little or no plastic region and break shortly beyond the yield point. Bending causes tension and compression on opposite sides of a piece of metal. Both forces cause the same kind of failure.

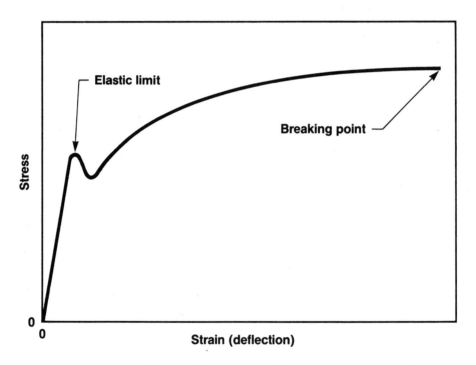

Fig. 15 Stress vs. strain curve

METAL FATIGUE

Metals fatigue and, unlike a fatigued human, a fatigued metal does not recover with rest. The fatigue limit is a measure of how often the metal can be stretched or bent back and forth in the elastic stress zone before it begins to crack and break. The closer the repeating stress is to the elastic limit (the boundary between elastic and plastic zones) the quicker it fatigues and breaks. The fatigue life of a metal depends on both the average stress and the change in stress. Static stress alone has no effect on fatigue. Static stress must be combined with dynamic stress to have an effect on fatigue.

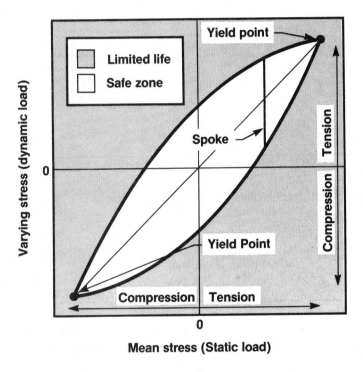

Fig. 16   Fatigue limit curve

The fatigue-life curve shown is for an ideal metal under stress. A material whose stress changes lie within this curve can withstand a nearly infinite number (millions) of stress cycles. The farther to the left or right of the center of the diagram the material is being stressed, the smaller is the permissible changing load for survival (e.g. a spoke working close to its yield point can carry only small loads without early fatigue failure.)

SPOKE FAILURE

Spokes fail from fatigue. They are subjected to fatiguing cycles of loading and unloading with each wheel rotation. The elbow and threads are affected most because they have the highest stress. Spoke fatigue results from the combination of static stress, the load carried, the distance traveled, and the number of spokes that share the work. Traveling long distances under heavy loads increases spoke fatigue.

Spokes seldom fail from overloads, except in unusual cases such as violent crashes. Even spokes that fail at moments of high stress are usually fatigue failures that were about to happen anyway. Failures that occur during a crash or on hitting a bump in the road are often only the "last straw" and should not be attributed to the event. Failures at the spoke elbow or threads are nearly always fatigue failures. In contrast a forced break will usually occur about 20 mm away from one of the spoke ends.

Tension tests using new spokes of various brands show that all high-quality spokes tested, butted and unbutted, break at more than three times the maximum tension they could encounter in use. The point of failure was, in all cases, neither in the threads nor at the elbow. These tests indicate that fatigue in its various stages plays a part in nearly every spoke failure.

Spoke failures from excessive pedaling torque are practically impossible. Those that occur during sprints or hard climbing are usually fatigued spokes that were already cracked and ready to break. Usually an undamaged new spoke will pull out of the rim or break its nipple before breaking from too much tension. Torque has a small fatigue effect on all spokes of a wheel but because average tension in the pulling spokes is slightly higher, their fatigue is slightly greater. However, because torque-induced tension changes are small compared to those from radial loads, fatigue effects are insignificant.

The rider's weight is the principal cause of spoke fatigue. Pedaling torque alone cannot affect fatigue, but added to radial loads, it does increase spoke stress. Even under the most severe pedaling, torque adds less than five percent to the stress from the rider's weight. Although tension changes from caliper brakes are sometimes larger than from pedaling torque, they have little effect because they do not occur at the load-affected zone and are not added to the principal stress.

Torque is not what causes more rear- than front-wheel spoke failures. These spokes fail more often because the rear wheel carries more weight, it receives more stress from the rigidity of the rear frame triangle, and, because it is asymmetric, it carries most of the load on half of its spokes which are at a higher tension than those of the front wheel. In contrast road shocks encountered by the front wheel are cushioned by the elasticity of the fork and top- and down-tubes, which absorb these forces in bending together, the frame and the rider's arm absorb most of the peak loads of the front wheel.

Asymmetry makes the spokes on the right side of the rear wheel about twice as tight as the ones on the left. The load carried by each side of the rear wheel is in direct proportion to the spoke tension. For loads, a 36-spoke rear wheel with a seven-speed gear cluster acts practically like an 18-spoke symmetric wheel. The greater the "dish" or asymmetry, the weaker the wheel and the more likely it is to collapse both from side loads and fatigue.

RIM FAILURE

Rims usually fail from crashes and road hazards such as potholes and rocks on the pavement. These often bend or dent the rim beyond repair. Rims also fail from fatigue. They develop cracks around the spoke holes and from one hole to the next. The cracks gradually weaken the wheel by releasing spoke tension. If the spokes are re-tensioned to re-true the wheel and bring it to proper tension, they will eventually pull out of the rim. This kind of failure does not cause wheel collapse because the spokes pull out one at a time and cause a loose, wobbly wheel. But riding a loose wheel invites wheel collapse from lateral loads.

WHEEL STRENGTH

Great strength and light weight are clearly desirable goals for every high performance wheel. These goals are mutually defeating; wheel design is the process of reconciling them. The ideal balance between strength and light weight is hard to find. To decide how strong a wheel needs to be and what components will give this strength requires an understanding of the effects of various spoke patterns, types of spokes, rims, and hubs. The durability of the wheel, its wind resistance, weight, and cost also require consideration. For the wheel builder ease of assembly may also be important.

To avoid the old pitfalls of poorly matched components, always keep in mind that it is better to be wrong in favor of strength rather than light weight. Understanding the tradeoff between spoke weight and rim weight will make achieving the right balance in your wheel easier. In view of the concepts presented in Part I, I think you will want to build standard wheels—standard wheels, but good ones.

STRENGTH AND DURABILITY

Strength is a measure of the greatest load the wheel can carry before it loses alignment. Durability is a measure of how far the wheel will travel before it loses alignment. The two usually go hand in hand — but not always.

A wheel can collapse when the spokes in the load-affected zone become loose. A load that will release tension in these spokes is roughly equal to the sum of the tension in four or five spokes. Therefore, the tighter the spokes (up to a point), the greater the wheel's load capacity. The wheel has both radial and lateral strength. These are closely related because most design features that make a wheel radially strong also make it laterally strong. This is also true for torsional strength, except with radial spoking.

A rigid rim combined with thin spokes gives the longest load-affected zone. By lengthening the load-affected zone a strong rim distributes loads over more spokes than would a weaker rim. Engaging more spokes in carrying loads makes the wheel stronger. Thin spokes have high elasticity, which permits them to absorb larger rim deflections without becoming slack. The more spokes that carry the load, the stronger the wheel. For carrying heavy loads, both a stronger rim and more spokes are advantageous.

Because wheel strength is closely related to the number of spokes in the load-affected zone, the number of spokes per inch remains about the same for different wheel sizes. A large wheel must have more spokes than a small wheel to achieve the same strength. High-wheeled bicycles, for example, require about 80 spokes instead of the usual 36. For a common 36-spoke wheel, the load-affected zone spans about four spokes.

If the spokes are tensioned to 100kg, a wheel could support approximately 400kg. This is considerably greater than the average rider's weight. However, 400 kg loads can occur when a wheel strikes a bump in the road. If this happens often, the nipples of the slack spokes can unscrew, releasing tension and affecting both wheel alignment and strength. Although radial overloads rarely cause wheel collapse, they can make the wheel lose alignment.

STIFFNESS

Stiffness is a measure of how hard it is to deflect the wheel or, more specifically, the ratio of load to displacement. Stiffness is not strength. For example, plaster is stiff but not very strong. Since wheel stiffness is so often discussed, I probably treat the various aspects of stiffness in more detail than they deserve. Wheel strength, and not stiffness, is the important consideration. If the wheel is strong enough for its intended use, then it is more than adequately stiff.

Since the stiffness of the frame, pedal cranks, and especially the tires is much lower than the wheel stiffness, differences among reasonably constructed wheels are imperceptible to a rider. The "liveliness" attributed to "stiff" wheels is an acoustic phenomenon that results largely from lightweight tires at high pressure and to a lesser degree from tight spokes. This mechanical resonance can be heard, and possibly felt in the handlebars, but it is not related to wheel stiffness. Liveliness is an indication of an un-dampened (low energy loss) wheel; it does not result from certain spoke patterns and has nothing to do with wheel stiffness.

The terms "stiffness" and "rigidity" are often used when people talk about bicycles. Unless these terms are defined, they are just as vague as the even more popular catchall term "responsiveness." These knowledgeable sounding technical words can be misleading. Stiffness alone is not the ultimate measure of a good wheel, but rather the balance of stiffness and elasticity that enables the wheel to carry loads, and absorb shock.

RADIAL STIFFNESS

Radial stiffness is a measure of the force required to deflect the rim radially. It is primarily influenced by the number and thickness of spokes. Spoke length also affects stiffness, but only in direct proportion to the length. A stiffer rim expands the load-affected zone so that loads are distributed over more spokes. This increases wheel stiffness.

Spoke patterns have little to no effect on stiffness. Spoke length differences among various spoke patterns are less than three percent. Since tire elasticity is about one hundred times greater, the elastic differences between the shortest and longest spokes amounts to less than 0.1 percent. Because butted spokes of different lengths are mostly made from the same spoke blanks, their elastic portions are equal so that length differences among butted spokes have even less effect than those of un-butted spokes.

LATERAL STIFFNESS

Lateral stiffness is a measure of the force required to deflect the rim to the side. Flange spacing, the rim stiffness, and the number and thickness of spokes all have an effect on lateral stiffness. The flange spacing has an effect because the horizontal component of the spoke tension restrains the lateral motion of the rim. The more the spokes pull to the sides, the greater is their lateral support.

As in radial stiffness, a stiffer rim affects lateral stiffness because it spreads the deflecting force over more spokes. Both an increased number of spokes and an increase in thickness increase lateral stiffness.

The asymmetry in rear wheels built for multi-speed gear clusters reduces lateral strength and stiffness against forces from the sprocket side. Five-speed wheels lack lateral strength but wheels with six- and seven-speed clusters are appreciably weaker.

A typical six-speed rear wheel is shown in cross-section. The horizontal scale in this graph (mm) is the same as for an actual hub. The curves show the change in spoke tension and the force required to displace the rim and cause these changes. The left spokes become slack for even small rim deflections to the left while the right spokes remain tight for the range of displacements shown. This wheel is twice as stiff for deflections to the right as to the left.

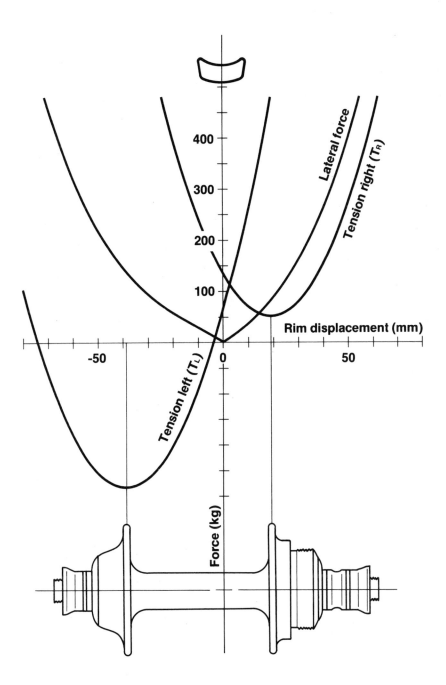

Fig. 17   Lateral force and spoke tension graph

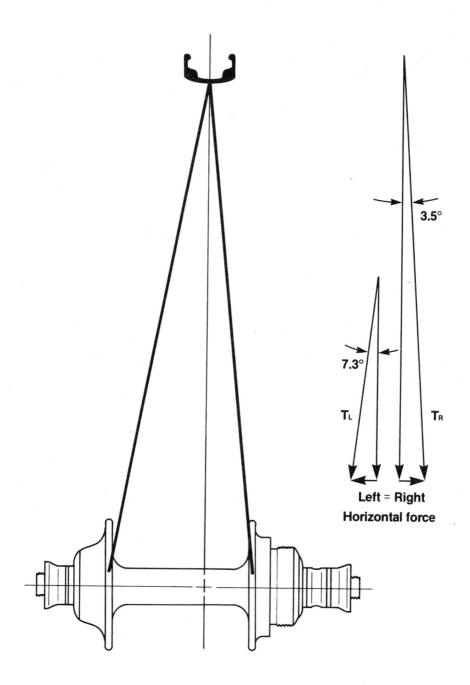

Fig. 18   Spoke tension in offset rear wheels

TORSIONAL STIFFNESS

Relative torsional stiffness is unimportant for most well built wheels but the effects of the spokes, rim and hub should be understood. The following discussion is not intended to help in selecting components, but instead aims to show the effects of various components even if they are insignificant.

Torsional stiffness is a measure of the torque required to rotate the hub relative to the rim. The angle of hub rotation with respect to the rim is called hub wind-up. Rim strength, spoke thickness, spoke pattern, and flange diameter all affect torsional stiffness. Rim strength plays only a minor role while spoke thickness has a squared effect: as the spoke diameter doubles, the stiffness increases fourfold. Hub diameter and spoke pattern also have a squared effect. For a given number of spokes, the torsional stiffness is proportional to the effective flange diameter squared.

The effective diameter of a flange depends on the spoke pattern. Radial spoking makes the effective diameter zero because the extended line of the spokes passes through the hub center while a crossed four pattern (for 36 spokes) gives full effect to the flange diameter because the spokes leave the hub at a right angle (tangent to it). The larger the flange, the greater the lever arm on which the spokes act. For the same wind-up, the larger flange also produces more movement (spoke stretch). Thus, a flange that is twice as large gives twice the spoke-tension change as well as providing twice the lever arm. This results in four times the torque for the same hub wind-up.

With the same rim and hub, different spoke patterns have the effect of changing the hub diameter. Radial spoking, for instance, reduces the effective diameter to zero while crossed four (with 36 spokes) makes the spokes tangent to the hub and gives the full effect of the hub diameter.

Radial spoking represents a special case because radial spokes pull directly across the hub and transmit no torque. However, even the slightest torque causes wind-up making radial spokes no longer radial. When torque is applied, all spoke tension acts directly on the offset caused by the wind-up to turn the wheel. With crossed spoking there is almost no wind-up; only the change in tension of pulling and pushing spokes moves the wheel. For radial spokes the effective hub diameter is the offset of the spoke line from the hub axis which, although small, produces enough torque to turn the wheel. Although it works, radial spoking has significant drawbacks that are described under radial spoking.

For most small flange hubs with 36 spokes, crossed three is a good reliable spoke pattern. However, crossed four will work on most 36 spoke rear hubs because they are large enough to prevent the spoke overlap that occurs on smaller hubs.

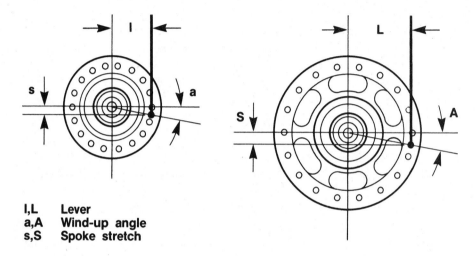

I,L   Lever
a,A   Wind-up angle
s,S   Spoke stretch

Fig. 19   Torsional stiffness and typical small and large flange hubs

ENOUGH STIFFNESS

In summary, stiffness is not a driving consideration in wheel design. Components and spoke patterns should be selected for strength and durability. A wheel that is strong enough to withstand the loads of its intended use is also stiff enough. Stiffness is often put forth as an excuse for peculiar designs —"it makes the wheel stiffer"— where durability should be the primary concern.

For example, some of the world's strongest cyclists ride the kilometer race on 24-spoke small-flange wheels with lightweight rims. This event requires precise control and enormous starting torque that exceeds nearly all stiffness and strength demands of other cycling. These racing wheels are adequately designed for their specific use but lack the long term durability of road wheels.

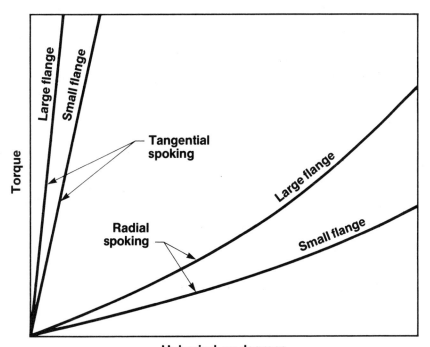

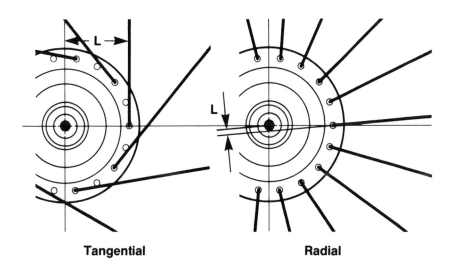

Fig. 20   Torque stiffness of crossed and radial spoking

COMPONENTS

Rims, hubs, spokes, and nipples are made in many shapes and from many materials. Rims are available in wood, steel, aluminum, titanium, composites and other materials. Spokes, although usually round and made of steel, are also available in oval and flat forms, and may soon be available in nonmetallic fibers. Material and design differences affect performance, durability, cost, ease of assembly, and appearance.

The hub's role in the structure of the wheel is simple because it needs only to have reasonable aluminum or similar flanges with the right size holes. The hub's complexity lies in its axle and bearings which have no effect the wheel structure. The important choices are the weight and shape of the rim, and the number and thickness of the spokes. This isn't a job of checking the correct box in the appropriate row and column because there are more rows and columns than you might suspect.

Select only fine quality components. Otherwise, when you are finished, you will discover that you did a high quality job but have mediocre wheels.

SPOKES

Spokes are the most highly stressed part of the wheel. They cause the most problems and they attract the most attention. Most spokes have a head and elbow at one end, and about eight millimeters of threads at the other. The majority of spokes have the same standard design, but spokes with special features such as aerodynamic shapes and elbowless ends are also available. Common round spokes can be found in four standard types: thin butted and unbutted, and thick butted and unbutted.

Spokes are made 1.8 and 2.0 mm thick (sometimes called 15 and 14 gauge; the larger the gauge number the thinner the spoke). The thickness of the midsection of some spokes is reduced by about 0.2 mm. These are called butted spokes, although they might better be called reduced spokes because they have been made thinner in the middle rather than thicker at the ends. The other important dimension, length, is measured from the inside of the elbow to the tip of the threaded end.

Most spokes have a round cross-section for a number of manufacturing and functional reasons. They are made from round wire and one end must be round for the thread. The opposite end must be round to allow the elbow to swivel in the flange to accommodate different spoke patterns. A round shape also makes wheel building easier because it resists twist when it is tightened.

STRAIGHT SPOKES

Straight gauge spokes are uniformly thick and are made from continuous wire. One end of the spoke blank is formed into a head which is bent into an elbow after the thread is rolled onto the other end. Spokes are entirely cold formed, which makes them tougher. The elbow bend is left greater than 90 degrees so that it can be set to the proper angle after insertion into the flange. Spokes on the inside and outside of a hub require different bends.

BUTTED SPOKES

Because stress is highest at the elbow and threads, spokes can be made thinner at mid-span without losing strength. These are butted spokes and are made by drawing the blanks through a special die that reduces their diameter. The reduction increases spoke elasticity, work-hardens the wire to increase strength and makes the finished spoke lighter.

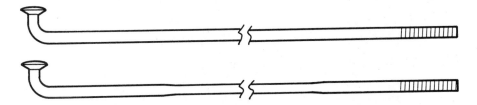

Fig. 21 Butted and un-butted spokes

ELBOW-LESS SPOKES

Spokes often fail at the elbow, so hubs that use straight, elbow-less spokes have been designed. In fact, some early high-wheeled bicycles used straight radial spokes with heads at the rim and threads in the hub. A recent variation on this design used straight spokes threaded at both ends with conventional nipples at the rim. Threaded hubs allow only the one spoke pattern for which they were designed. Besides expense, their main failing is that spokes which break off in the hub cannot be removed.

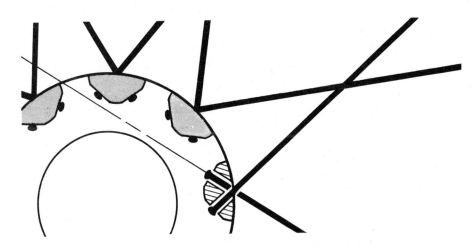

Fig. 22 Hub with elbow-less spokes

Another more promising design, found on some motorcycles, uses spokes similar to the conventional kind, but without an elbow bend. These spokes project through the rim of cup-shaped flanges (Fig. 22) to the rim where they are tightened by standard nipples. Although this design also allows only one spoke pattern, its main drawback for bicycles is that it requires a larger, heavier hub.

FLAT AND OVAL SPOKES

Flattened spokes are made to reduce wind drag but their resistance to twist is so poor that they are difficult to tighten without twisting them into a corkscrew shape. Twist continues to be a problem in use because the spokes are subjected to unscrewing forces from road shock. With so little torsional strength they gradually turn crosswise to the wind and need to be continually adjusted.

Both oval and flattened spokes are made from unbutted spoke blanks and have as good or better tensile strength in the flattened part as the original spoke. Although they are strong in tension, their poor resistance to twist and the need for special flange holes make them unsatisfactory for general cycling use.

OTHER SPECIAL SPOKES

Extra thick mountain bike spokes that neck down to a standard 2.0 mm threaded end give the appearance of great strength. Exactly the opposite is true because these spokes concentrate stress in the threads, a vulnerable zone even on conventional spokes. Conventional 2.0 mm spokes are strong enough. The fear that they are too weak may have come from early mountain bikes which used low quality 26 inch wheels from inexpensive balloon-tired bicycles.

Headless zigzag-bent spokes for insertion "head first" are not the ideal solution they seem to be. They allow spokes next to the freewheel to be replaced easily, and flat spokes of this type do not require slotted flanges. However, the cost of getting rid of the spoke head is that these spokes worm their way out of their flanges under high tension. If tension is kept low to avoid these failures, the wheel strength will be compromised.

SPOKE THICKNESS AND PERFORMANCE

Butted spokes, although more expensive to make and slightly more difficult to true, give more durable wheels. They are more elastic than un-butted spokes because their thin mid-sections stretch more and they can be made just as tight as unbutted spokes. Under load, they resist loosen-ing better than straight spokes. Their resilience helps the rim distribute loads over more spokes and reduces peak stress changes. Butted spokes are lighter without giving up any strength. Their ends are identical to those of straight spokes while the mid-sections are strengthened by diameter reduction.

Unbutted spokes usually cost less than butted spokes because they are simpler to manufacture. Their stiffness also makes wheel truing easier. Because they have greater torsional and tensile stiffness than butted spokes, they twist very little and can be adjusted accurately and easily. The greater stiffness reduces elastic interactions among spokes which, in turn, simplifies truing. Unbutted spokes are often used for racing because with them wheels can be built rapidly, and when a spoke breaks wheel alignment suffers less than with butted spokes.

The greater stiffness of straight spokes subjects them to higher stress by concentrating loads over fewer spokes. Higher stress changes give them a shorter fatigue life. Their stiffness allows them to become slack more easily, which permits the nipple to unscrew unless they are secured by one of the following methods. If the wheels use tubular tires, a bit of rim glue in the nipple sockets will secure the nipples. For clinchers, which use no glue, a non-hardening thread-locking adhesive or a sticky spoke thread lubricant can be used. Crimping nipples is not effective and damages them. If the rim and spokes are properly matched, the wheel should stay true without adhesives.

SPOKE THREADS

Most spokes, both 1.8 and 2.0 mm, have 56 threads per inch (TPI). Some 1.8 mm spokes have been made with a finer 0.4 mm pitch thread that has several advantages. Finer thread allows finer adjustment. Because it advances less each turn, a spoke with finer thread tightens with less torque, thereby reducing spoke twist. This spoke is stronger because its thread grooves are not as deep. And most important, finer thread prevents the common mistake of using 2.0 mm nipples on 1.8 mm spokes which strip out when they are tensioned.

Spoke threads are formed by rolling, not cutting. The spoke is rolled between two flat thread dies with thread profiles on them. The process is similar to rolling modeling clay into a rope between your hands. The rolled thread is stronger than a cut thread because it is forged into the material instead of being cut. A rolled thread is easily recognized because it is larger than the spoke diameter.

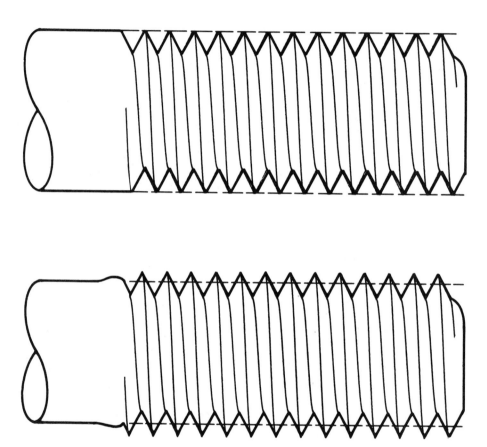

Fig. 23   Cut threads and rolled threads

SPOKE TWIST

Spokes are, in effect, very long screws. Because they are so long they act like long springy torsion bars, especially when they are made very tight. 2.0 mm spokes have about fifty percent greater torsional stiffness than 1.8 mm spokes, and unbutted spokes have about fifty percent greater torsional stiffness than butted spokes.

When a spoke nipple is turned, it tends to twist the spoke. This torque, the windup torque on the spoke, has two components, thread ramp and friction. The steepness of the thread is function of the thread pitch and the thread diameter. It resists spoke tightening and helps loosening, and you can't do anything about it. The friction component is dependent only on thread diameter and lubrication, and it can be reduced significantly by proper lubrication.

SPOKE MATERIALS

Although titanium and aluminum spokes have been made, they have less strength and poorer fatigue resistance than steel spokes. Steel is less expensive than other materials and it wears better against the hub. Most spokes are either stainless steel, or steel with plating to prevent corrosion. Chrome- or nickel-plated spokes are brighter than cadmium- or zinc-plated spokes, but they rust more easily.

Wheels with plated spokes are difficult to re-true after exposure to wet weather because their threads rust making nipples difficult to turn. Stainless steel spokes, although more expensive, are nearly as bright as chrome-plated spokes and are easier to maintain. Plated and stainless spokes can be made equally strong, but lasting wheels are usually built with stainless spokes that do not deteriorate from exposure to weather.

SPOKE NIPPLES

Spoke nipples are both the anchor at the end of the spoke and the means for truing the wheel. Most spoke nipples are brass, although some are made of aluminum or steel. Aluminum is one-third as heavy as brass, but because aluminum is soft, great care must be taken not to round the nipples with the spoke wrench or to strip the threads. Steel, although stronger than brass, rusts easily. Nipples with rusted threads are of no use if the wheel needs truing. Brass is the best material for nipples because it acts as a bearing, allowing the nipple to turn smoothly on the steel spoke.

Brass nipples are usually plated with cadmium or nickel to improve their appearance and prevent tarnishing. Plating could protect the outside of steel nipples but would not prevent rusted threads. The threads of brass nipples are cut after plating. Subsequent weathering of the threads causes only a thin layer of tarnish which does not affect their function.

NIPPLE LENGTHS

Nipples are made in various lengths, primarily to suit different rim thicknesses. Most wooden rims, for instance, required 25mm long nipples to reach through the rim. Nipples must be long enough to expose flanks for a spoke wrench where they protrude from the rim. But regardless of length, nipples usually have no more than 20 threads at the head end and a smooth hole for the remainder of their length.

HEX HEAD NIPPLES

Some automatic wheel truing machines use spoke nipples that have hexagonal heads instead of the more common rounded heads that have a screw slot. In these machines the heads of all the nipples are engaged simultaneously by socket wrenches and are tightened until the tension and the alignment, measured by sensors, are within a specified tolerance. These spoke nipples also have flat flanks so that a standard spoke wrench can be used for subsequent truing.

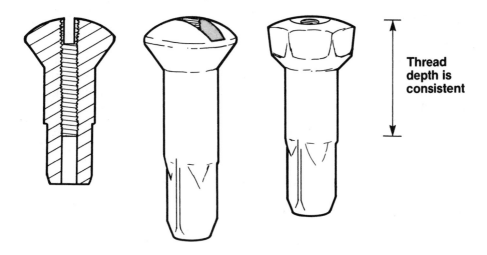

Thread depth is consistent

Fig. 24 Nipple threads and shapes

RIMS

The rim appears mainly to serve as a mount for the tire and a disc for braking. However, it has an important structural role in the wheel. It supports the combined tension of the spokes and distributes wheel loads. It must be elastic enough to absorb shock loads, yet stiff enough to distribute them over several spokes. It must be strong radially, laterally and in twist. As part of the braking system it must convert kinetic energy to heat, absorb and dissipate this heat, and resist wear from the friction of the brake pads.

RIM DESIGN

Rims are made in various shapes, from simple U-shaped sections to closed, rectangular-box sections. For narrow clincher rims, a cross-section with more strength than a simple channel is achieved by adding a hollow section under the bed of the rim. This greatly improves strength with little additional weight. Rim strength is needed to distribute lateral and radial loads among the spokes.

Extruded aluminum alloy rims provide the best combination of light weight, high strength, good ductility, corrosion resistance and cost. Ductility describes how well a rim can bend in a crash without breaking. Aluminum alloy makes a more ductile rim than most other materials except steel. However, steel rims are heavier and are used primarily in inexpensive bicycles to reduce cost.

The ideal cross section for a rim is a rectangular tube, the structural form that has the greatest bending and torsional strength. A tire cannot be mounted on this ideal shape, but tubular tire rims with a U-shaped rectangular cross section come close to this ideal. Clincher rims cannot be as ideally shaped because they must be open to accept the tire and tube, but with good design some of them are nearly as good as rims for tubular tires. Aluminum rims are extruded like toothpaste through a forming die into straight rods and are then shaped into hoops.

Fig. 25   Rim cross sections

AERODYNAMIC RIMS

Streamlined rims have deep, rounded "V" shapes. Most of these rims are heavier and more rigid than their conventional counterparts. Their braking surfaces are not perpendicular to the surface of the brake pads and they have no reinforcement for spoke nipples. Structurally they give a strong wheel but their aerodynamic advantage is achieved at the expense of these deficiencies.

RIM SPOKE HOLES

Aluminum rims are too soft to support concentrated spoke forces directly at the nipples. Steel ferrules are crimped into the spoke holes of aluminum rims to reinforce them and to prevent nipples from gouging the rim when they are tightened. Steel washers can also be used, but these are uncommon. Hollow cross section rims often have steel sockets that distribute the spoke loads to both the inner and outer walls of the rim. This method of spoke support permits thinner walls and lighter rims. Rims without sockets to distribute the load to both walls often crack with use around the spoke holes.

Steel washers, even thick ones, are relatively low in bending strength compared to a deep socket. Therefore, washers must be nearly as heavy as sockets to carry the same load. Since only one wall of the rim supports the spokes, this wall must be thick to give the same strength as a thin wall in a rim with sockets. Rims with washers are only lighter than rims with sockets when weighed without their washers.

RIM JOINT

Rims are formed from straight material and have a joint where the hoop is closed. Most solid section rims are welded, as are some hollow aluminum rims. For rims that have a large hollow cross-section, however, welding is not only difficult and expensive, but unnecessary. The most common method for joining hollow rims is with a closely fitting plug inserted at the joint. This type of joint resists all forces except tension (pulling apart). Spoke tension ensures that the joint always remains in compression (pushed together). Most unspoked rims with the insert type joint can be pulled apart by hand.

RIM MATERIALS

Rims have been made of wood, steel, aluminum alloys and other materials. The shape and function of the rim makes aluminum alloy the best material. It has good thermal conductivity and excellent strength and ductility. A steel rim of the same bending strength and weight as aluminum would have such thin walls that it could not support the forces at the spoke nipples. The wall thickness of steel required to withstand local concentrated loads makes steel rims appreciably heavier than aluminum rims.

The light weight of aluminum permits thicker walls that support the spokes and absorb road shocks without denting. Its toughness enables aluminum to bend in a crash without breaking and exposing dangerous edges. Also, brakes work better on wet aluminum rims than on wet steel ones. Although these features make aluminum an excellent material for rims, steel (due to its lower cost) will remain popular for less expensive wheels.

Wooden rims are strong and light, and are ideal for gluing on tubular tires. Since wood is a good insulator, heat produced by braking will not soften the tire glue and cause tire creep. However, the disadvantages of wood outweigh these positive features. Wood is brittle and will not tolerate denting or partial failure. Thus, rim failure usually results in collapse and dangerous splinters. Distortion and loss of spoke tension caused by moisture make repeated truing necessary. Low thermal conductivity keeps wooden rims from absorbing heat. With wood, the friction surface becomes so hot that brake pads burn away rapidly. In addition, wooden rims require greater braking force than metal rims because high temperature reduces the coefficient of friction.

WOOD-FILLED RIMS FOR TUBULAR TIRES

Instead of sockets or washers, wooden filler pieces have been placed inside rims. These pieces have the same effect as the steel sockets but require much smaller holes in the metal. Because the holes need to be only large enough to fit the shafts of the nipples, less material is removed from the rim. These rims can have very thin walls and still give adequate strength. Wood-filled rims are extremely light but they have disadvantages. First, no wood is strong enough for this job. Second, the effects of the spoke loads and moisture cause a loss in spoke tension and, consequently, in strength and alignment.

Wood-filled rims present other problems. The nipples cannot swivel in the rim to accommodate different spoke angles. Therefore, spokes may bend excessively at the nipple. The holes must be drilled in the rim at angles to match a specific spoke pattern. Wood rims and wood-filled rims require long nipples. They must reach from the bed of the tire through the rim to expose flanks that can engage a spoke wrench. Long nipples often bind while being turned, making wheel truing more difficult, and they are heavier than short nipples. Because they have these disadvantages, wood-filled (and wooden) rims are rarely used now.

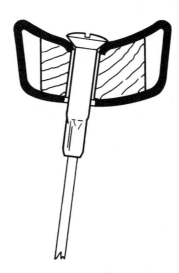

Fig. 26   Wood filled rim

ANODIZED ALUMINUM RIMS

Aluminum naturally and rapidly forms a self-sealing oxide that protects its silvery surface. This characteristic does not protect it against the opaque blotches caused by more aggressive chemicals such as the salts and acids found on wet city streets. However, with artificial oxidation, aluminum can build up a sufficient layer to protect itself even against harsh environments.

Anodizing is an electrolytic process that oxidizes aluminum in an acid bath. The oxide is transparent, but as its thickness increases it becomes grey or brown depending on the alloying metals in the aluminum. The oxide is a glassy, porous and hard but brittle coating with thickness up to about 0.3 mm. It rises out of the metal as much as it grows into the surface. Dyes can be added to give anodized surfaces a wide range of colors that mask the dull color of the oxide.

Hard anodizing is a similar process performed in a chilled bath with additives to control porosity and oxide growth. It has a thickness of up to about 0.15 mm. Hard anodizing can also be dyed but its natural olive green color lends itself best to dark colors.

Anodized rims have some disadvantages. Although anodizing prevents corrosion and makes coloring possible, its structure and thermal resistance reduce brake efficiency. Thermal resistance causes brake pads to become hotter reducing their coefficient of friction. The hard surface, if it is thick, can initiate cracks in the rim at the spoke holes. The oxide is brittle and cracks easily at places where the surface of the rim is in tension from bending.

Some aluminum rims are treated with chromate conversion. This electrolytic process converts the surface of the aluminum to aluminum chromate, giving a bright silvery finish that has durable corrosion resistance. Aluminum chromate is not an insulator and does not have the brittleness of anodizing, but it is only available in clear and yellow.

BRAKING CHARACTERISTICS

Braking efficiency of a rim is characterized by its thermal capacity and conductivity, its surface structure, and its ability to hold moisture. Various rim materials have different braking characteristics. With a suitable brake pad, dry steel rims have the best braking performance. However, wet steel rims brake poorly. Although wood rims are never very good, at least they do not become much worse when wet. Aluminum is nearly as good as steel when dry, but better than wood when wet. Anodizing on aluminum rims reduces braking performance.

BRAKE HEATING

Metal rims can become hotter than boiling water while braking on long descents. Heat is generated in the brake pad and is transferred into the rim. Since the rim is many times harder than the brake pad, does not deform or wear except from occasional bits of road debris. All mechanical action that generates heat takes place in the softer pad material.

During braking the back of the brake pad remains cool to the touch because it conducts heat poorly. The heat that is generated in the pad transfers to the rim where it diffuses because the rim has good thermal conductivity, good heat capacity, and a large cooling surface. During braking, the face of the pad becomes hot and is cooled by the rim. Because a wooden rim is an insulator, little heat is transferred to it and the brake pad melts or burns.

HUBS

The hub may appear as the most important part of the wheel because it is centrally located with the rest of the wheel rotating around it. The hub is important but its design has been perfected to a point where, except for the bearings and freewheel, it requires little attention. Nevertheless, there are a number of important considerations in selecting a hub.

HUB DESIGN

Hubs have flanges in which the spokes are anchored. For a given number of spokes a certain flange size is necessary to accommodate the spoke holes and still leave material between them to support the load. The combination of space for holes and space for supporting material determines the smallest diameter for a flange. For an aluminum-alloy hub the space between spokes should be at least half again as wide as the spoke hole diameter. Because aluminum hubs have less than one-fourth the strength of the spoke material and about twice its thickness, this spacing is about the minimum necessary for a reasonable safety margin.

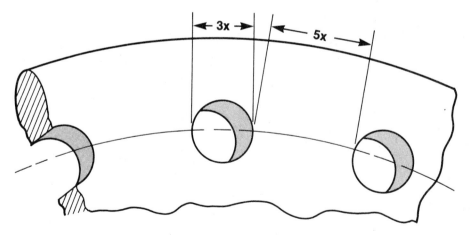

Fig. 27   Hole spacing in flange

The flange material must be strong enough to support the spoke loads, yet softer than the spokes. Although steel is stronger than aluminum, it does not support spokes as well because it is too hard. Aluminum alloy has adequate strength, is lighter than steel, and is soft enough to allow spokes to bed into the flange to give good support. The flange material on which the spokes bear is stressed enough to make it conform to the spokes. The material must be soft enough to yield under point loads of the spoke yet be strong enough to support the spoke tension.

To give better spoke support and to allow easier spoke insertion, the edges of the spoke holes are usually beveled. Some aluminum-alloy hubs are made with trumpet shaped holes to match the curvature of the spoke elbow. However, a plain hole in which the spoke can form its own contour gives better support than a pre-formed radius. The contours formed by the spokes are visible on the flanges of a an un-radiused aluminum hub after un-spoking.

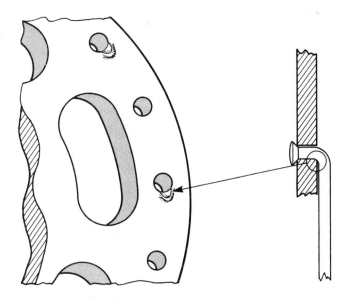

Fig. 28   Spoke seating in the flange

SMALL- AND LARGE-FLANGE HUBS

Hubs are made with small flanges or large flanges (low-flange and high-flange). The designations are arbitrary but generally large-flange hubs have a flange diameter appreciably larger than needed for 36 spokes. Small-flange hubs for front wheels usually have flanges about 40mm in diameter which is about as small as spoke spacing permits. Some small-flange front hubs, however, cannot be spoked tangentially with more than 32 spokes without spoke overlap. Flanges of rear hubs must be larger than front hubs because the spoke holes must lie outside the diameter of a standard freewheel thread.

For convenience, hubs with the same size flanges, front and rear, have been made to use the same length spokes. In this arrangement the front hub is as large as the rear hub rather than as small as possible.

The main functional difference among hubs with different flange diameters is their torque stiffness. Because most large-flange hubs are about 50 percent larger in diameter than small-flange rear hubs, they are about two and a quarter times stiffer torsionally. For a given spoke pattern, torque stiffness increases as the square of the flange diameter: if the flange diameter doubles, the stiffness increases four times.

The squared effect arises because the radius appears twice as a factor in the torque stiffness expression. It appears as the lever arm and in the amount of spoke stretch. Therefore, large-flange hubs can reduce torque loads in the spokes with small increases in diameter. It is important to remember that in most wheels torque loads are already adequately supported by small-flange hubs. So using large flange hubs provides no functional advantage and has the disadvantage of adding weight.

Tandem bicycles are an exception. With 36 spokes or less, tandem wheels require large-flange hubs to withstand the torque of two riders. And to support the additional weight, durable tandem wheels require at least 48 spokes which can only be accommodated by larger flanges.

In addition to their use on tandems, large flange hubs are sometimes seen on track racing bicycles where, by tradition, torque was said to be so great that such hubs were essential. In fact, the tradition probably originated before the days of reliable spokes. Because the flanges of these hubs are larger than the sprockets, they allow spokes to be replaced without removing the sprocket. This is not true for most road wheels.

FLANGE DIAMETER AND TORSIONAL STIFFNESS
Common large-flange hubs spoked tangentially are about twice as stiff torsionally as common low-flange hubs. Such low-flange hubs require

about twenty meter-kilograms (mkg) per degree of hub wind-up. This means that the average rider, using a two-to-one chain ratio and 170 mm cranks, would have to press on the pedals with 250kg to wind-up a small-flange hub one degree, or about 520kg (more than half a ton) for a large-flange hub.

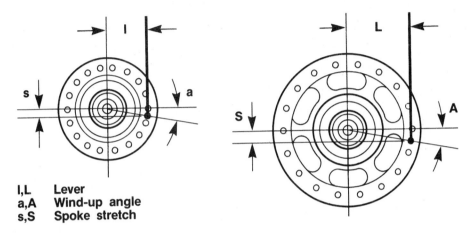

I,L   Lever
a,A   Wind-up angle
s,S   Spoke stretch

Fig. 29   Torsional stiffness and flange size

It is evident from this comparison that small-flange hubs provide adequate torsional strength and stiffness. There is no need to use large-flange hubs for greater torsional stiffness, but their reduction of torque-induced spoke loads might improve fatigue life slightly. However, with larger flanges the spoke angle at the rim becomes less perpendicular causing spokes to bend at the nipple. This bend increases failures at the threads and probably cancels any gains from reduced torque loads. To avoid this problem, large-flange hubs are often spoked in a less than fully tangential pattern.

HIGH-LOW REAR HUBS

Hubs with a high flange on the right and a low flange on the left have been made in an attempt to balance the offset in multi-speed rear wheels. This arrangement has no effect except with radial spoking. Offset, which is the principle problem in rear wheels, can be reduced only by moving the freewheel farther away from the wheel centerline, or by narrowing the flange spacing. Offset is undesireable because it causes large left-to-right differences in spoke tension and makes the wheel more likely to collapse from side loads from the right. Bringing the left flange closer to the center improves the balance of spoke tension but only at the expense of reducing lateral strength on both sides of the wheel.

The larger diameter of the right flange can help balance tension by about five percent, but only if the spokes are radial. With tangential spoking, no improvement is achieved. The large flange, however, makes spoke insertion on the low side difficult. High-lows cannot reduce the vertical load that is the principal cause of spoke failures. Torque loads have so little effect on fatigue that high-low hubs offer no improvement over conventional hubs.

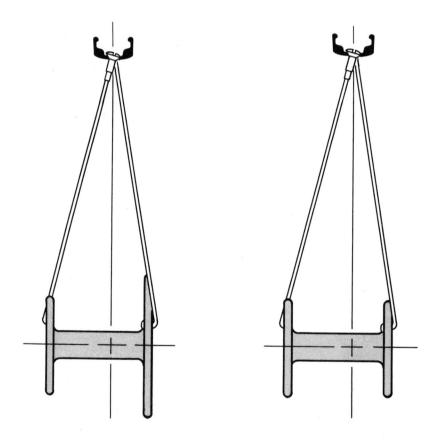

Fig. 30 High-low-flange vs. low-flange hub, both spoked tangentially

TORSIONAL STIFFNESS OF THE REAR HUB

Because torque transmission is not a problem, the following discussion is of more theoretical than practical interest. With tangential (crossed) spoking most wheels, whether large- or small-flange, are more than strong enough to transmit any torque encountered.

Some of the torque from the drive side of the hub is transmitted through the hub shaft to the opposite flange. The torsional stiffness of this shaft determines how much torque will be transmitted. The shaft in the center of common aluminum alloy rear hubs is relatively weak and has a torsional stiffness of about three meter-kilograms per degree of twist. This is considerably less than the torque stiffness of the spoke pattern, but it is enough to transmit thirteen percent of the torque in a tangentially spoked small-flange hub. In a large-flange hub only seven percent of the torque is transmitted through the shaft because, in comparison with the small-flange hub, the effective spoke stiffness is much greater.

With high-low-flange hubs, where the right flange is larger than the left flange, nearly all the torque goes to the spokes on the right side of the wheel.

Some hubs with large-diameter shafts have such a high torsional stiffness that the torque is transmitted almost equally to both sides of the wheel. This design feature makes small-flange hubs torsionally as stiff as conventional large-flange hubs. Track racing hubs, that accommodate only a single sprocket rather than multiple sprockets, have their flanges so widely spaced that their shafts transmit less than five percent of the driving torque to the left side of the wheel.

WHEEL DESIGN

Wheel design consists mainly of selecting the best components for your use. There is not much to decide in the way of spoke patterns, unless you are limited by available spoke lengths. It should be no surprise that tangential spoking is the best for all wheels with hardly an exception. It is only a matter of convenience how close the spokes are to being fully tangential. For instance, with 36 spokes cross three is nearly tangential and cross four is fully tangential.

It may be futile to suggest the ordinary but let me try to persuade you that just to build a conventional standard 36 spoke wheel is not a trivial task if a durable wheel is your goal. Cyclists who choose to build wheels often want something more than ordinary wheels. It may be a disappointment to discover that "it's all been done before" and that today's conventional wheels are a result of a hundred years of refinement. Your true contribution is to build conventional wheels exceptionally well.

NUMBER OF SPOKES

The number of spokes affects the strength and the durability of the wheel. The 36-spoke wheel has become a standard in racing and touring because it is a good balance between durability and light weight. With increased concern about wind drag 32- and 28-spoke wheels have become more common. Although an extra-light wheel with few spokes may survive on the road for a while, experienced riders usually choose wheels for durability.

Spokes at the top of the wheel move twice as fast through the wind as the bicycle so their drag is significant. The more spokes the more drag. Reducing wind drag is the primary reason for using fewer spokes. For events such as the kilometer time trial, wheels with 24 spokes were common until disc wheels were approved. Reducing the number of spokes to save weight is not an effective approach. Lighter rims and thin-butted spokes do a better job.

SPOKE PATTERNS

A spoke pattern is defined by the number of times each spoke crosses adjacent spokes on its way from the hub to the rim. Cross zero, for instance, is a radial pattern. Radial spokes project straight out on a line from the axle to the rim. Crossed spokes lie more or less tangent to the flange and cross over one or more adjacent spokes between the hub and rim. They project from the flanges both clockwise and counter-clockwise so that they cross one another. There are also mixed patterns called "crow's-foot," with both radial and crossed spokes.

RADIAL SPOKING

Radial spokes carry loads as well as crossed spokes can, but they cannot transmit torque. They can only transmit torque after the hub rotates ahead of the rim, making the spokes no longer truly radial. This wind-up produces a small lever on which spoke tension can act to produce torque. This lever is the distance between the axis of the hub and the extended axis of the no-longer-radial spokes. The driving torque is the product of this small offset and the tension of all the spokes.

In a radial rear wheel, the wind-up that occurs while riding is small (less than two degrees.) However, this motion increases spoke fatigue while spoke rotation in the flange causes wear. As radial spokes wind up under torque, they become appreciably tighter and cause excessive rim stress. Loose spoking could reduce wind-up induced tension, but then the wheel could not carry loads.

There is another reason why wheels should not be spoked radially: high radial stress can cause flange failure. Even though they transmit no torque, front wheels should be spoked tangentially. Aluminum-alloy hubs can break out at the spoke holes causing wheel collapse. These failures usually take time to occur as the flange fatigues. Some lightweight hubs carry specific warnings against radial spoking.

Radial spoking has no aerodynamic advantage over other patterns because, when seen from the direction of travel, the spokes beat into the wind the same as in any other pattern. At the point where the most wind strikes them, the spokes in any pattern lie behind one another to the same extent. Without resorting to disc wheels or flat spokes, the right way to reduce drag is to use fewer spokes.

CROSSED SPOKING

Crossed or tangential spoking is used to transmit torque. The term "tangential" refers to the way the spokes project from the flanges. The spokes turn the hub by pulling on a lever equal to the effective radius of the flange. The more tangential the spoke pattern is to the flange, the greater the effective flange radius. This radius is the distance between the spoke axis and the hub axis. It is the lever that enables the cross-spoked wheel to transmit torque with lower stress than a radially-spoked wheel. With spokes nearly tangent to the flanges, adjacent spokes pull in opposite directions and produce little radial stress on the flange. This lower stress, in contrast to the much higher stress of radial spoking, reduces the possibility of flange failure.

NUMBER OF SPOKE CROSSINGS

The number of spoke crossings in a wheel is defined as the number of spokes from the same flange that each spoke crosses between the hub and rim. The maximum number of crossings is produced when the spokes lie most nearly tangent to the flange. This number can be determined by dividing the number of spokes by nine. For example, for a 32-spoke wheel the maximum number is three. If this number is exceeded, the effective flange diameter will be reduced and spokes will cross over the heads of others, causing overlap.

If the diameter is very large or very small, the number of spoke crossings must be reduced to avoid interference between the spokes at the flanges. When an extra-large-flange hub, such as one with a hub brake, is spoked with the usual maximum crossings, spokes will reach beyond the tangent point on the flange and interfere with adjacent spokes. When spokes interfere with adjacent spoke heads they receive an additional bend that increases stress and makes spoke replacement difficult.

INTERLACED SPOKES

Spokes in a crossed pattern are usually interlaced. Spokes coming from between the flanges are laid over ones from outside the flanges at their last crossing before reaching the rim. Interlaced spokes take up each other's slack during severe radial loading and prevent nipple rotation. Radial spokes cannot be interlaced and therefore, lose alignment more easily. Interlacing also gives more clearance between the spokes and the derailleur on rear wheels.

IDENTICAL AND MIRROR-IMAGE SPOKING

Wheels with crossed spoke patterns can be built with the left and right sides identical to one another or as mirror-image opposites. This design feature only affects rear wheels where torque is transmitted. The difference between mirror image and identical spoking is so insignificant that it should be viewed as an academic subject of little practical value.

In a wheel with identical spoking, both flanges have the pulling spokes on the left (or right) side rather than between them (or outside of them). During torque transmission the pulling and pushing spokes of each flange exert a lateral force toward the pulling side. Although this motion is small, it can move the rim laterally as much as one millimeter with each pedal stroke.

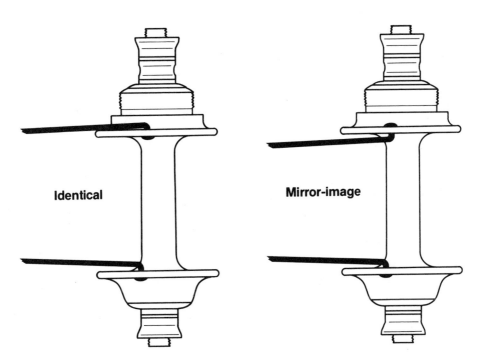

Identical   **Mirror-image**

Fig. 31 Identical and mirror image spoking

In a wheel with mirror-image spoking, all the spokes coming from between the flanges are the same kind, either pulling or pushing. During torque transmission, the pulling and pushing spokes of each flange exert a lateral force in opposite directions and tend to cancel each other. The spokes on the left oppose the lateral force from spokes on the right rather than reinforcing it as with identical spoking. These lateral forces would be perfectly balanced if each flange transmitted half of the torque.

Tension changes resulting from pedaling cause an interlaced spoke crossing to move toward the side of the pulling spoke. At the crossing point, the tighter (pulling) spoke straightens while the other spoke bends more. This moves the crossing point in or out depending on the spoking. If the derailleur is close to the spokes and the pulling spoke comes from the outside of the flange, clearance will be reduced when torque is transmitted. Pulling spokes coming from the inside of the flange would draw the spokes away from the derailleur. To improve rear derailleur clearance rear wheels should be spoked mirror-image with the pulling spokes coming from between the flanges.

COMBINED SPOKING PATTERNS

Wheels can be laced in spoke patterns that combine radial and crossed spokes. These patterns are interesting in appearance but have no measurable advantages over common crossed spoke patterns. For example, the "crow's-foot" pattern has two-thirds crossed spokes and one-third radial. The pattern is formed by a one- or two-crossed pattern with a radial spoke between each pair of opposing spokes. This pattern can only be used on wheels with spokes in multiples of six. Spoking the left and right sides differently on similar size flanges has no advantages. Such left-right combinations are usually used with hub brakes where flange diameters are different. For these hubs it is best to use fewer crossings on the larger flange so that the spokes do not enter the rim at too great an angle.

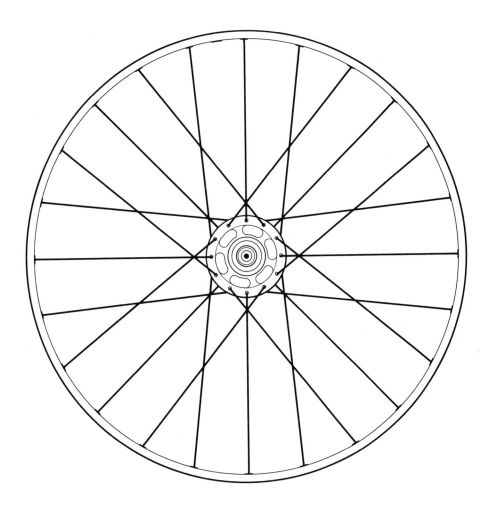

Fig. 32   24 spoke crow's foot pattern

SPOKE TENSION

The correct tension for a wheel is a balance between rim strength and wheel stability. For greatest strength, spokes should be as tight as the rim permits. In practice, however, spokes should be slightly looser because when they are at the limit, failure of a single spoke can severely deform the rim. Because the greatest force in the rim is compression from the tension of the spokes, failure from too much tension turns the wheel into a pretzel shape. If the spoke nipples are lubricated properly and turn freely, spokes can easily be tightened beyond the strength of the rim.

Even though spokes are seldom tightened to more than one third of their breaking tension, they occasionally fail during tensioning. Torque required to turn spoke nipples increases with tension, and if the nipples are not well-lubricated, the combined stress of tension and twist can cause spoke failure. The combined stress has a greater effect than the sum of the individual stresses.

During normal use, spoke tension is the principal load on the rim. Although the tension in individual spokes changes considerably in use, the average tension of all the spokes remains nearly constant and, therefore, so does the rim load caused by this tension. As a result, spoke tension near the limit of rim strength does not overload the rim in use. The tension limit is best determined experimentally by repeatedly stress-relieving the spokes.

IMPROVING THE SPOKE LINE

In the cross-spoked wheel, the spokes bend as they enter the hub and the rim. These bends should be supported at the hub by the flange and at the rim by the nipple. The unsupported spoke shaft should lie in a straight line between the last points of contact at the hub and rim. If there is an unsupported bend in a spoke, it will flex with changing loads causing fatigue and early failure.

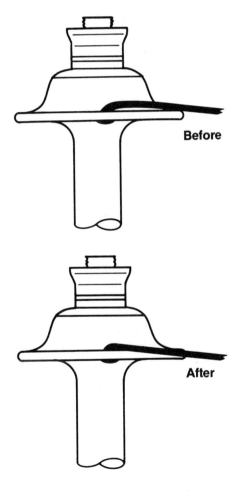

Fig. 33 Spoke line at the hub

The ideal spoke line is the line that a fine thread would take if substituted for the spoke. It would lie flush against supporting surfaces of the flange and nipple, and would lie in a straight line between. The spoke line is improved by bending the outer spokes against the flange with the thumbs. If the nipples do not swivel sufficiently to match the spoke angle, grasp crossing spokes in pairs near the rim and squeeze them together. These spoke adjustments must be performed with care to prevent over-correction.

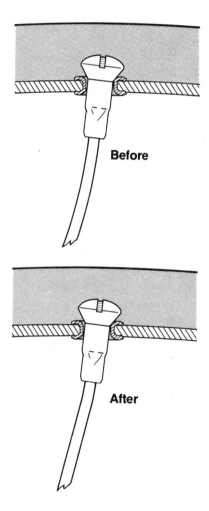

Fig. 34   Spoke line at the rim

STRESS-RELIEVING

After improving the spoke line, and when the wheel is well trued and tensioned, the spokes may appear to be in perfect alignment. However, some of the spokes have a good line at the elbow and rim only because they are tensioned. They were at the yield point when they were bent into place and with the addition of tension they are sure to remain at yield. Spokes stressed to the yield point have a short fatigue life although they have no visible signs of high stress. These invisible stresses must be relieved to make the wheel durable.

HOW STRESS-RELIEVING WORKS

Stress-relieving can be regarded as improving the spoke line at a microscopic level. This process momentarily increases the spoke tension of the misaligned spoke beyond the yield point where it bends. When the yield point is exceeded, the spoke takes a permanent set. The wheel may lose tension during stress-relieving, but not because the spokes stretch when they are stressed. Any length change occurring at the high stress points is microscopic. Loss of spoke tension comes from the spoke elbow seating into the flange. When the over-tension is released, the stress at the bends drops below the yield point and the peak stress is relieved.

Stress-relieving also provides an accurate method for determining the maximum safe spoke tension for a wheel. If the wheel is too tight, it will warp during stress-relieving. A properly tensioned wheel must withstand a firm grasp on two spoke pairs with only slight loss of alignment. When testing a wheel's tension, be careful at first not to squeeze the spokes too hard. If the wheel is too tight, it will distort easily.

HOW TO RELIEVE STRESS

Spokes are best stress-relieved by grasping the most nearly parallel spoke pairs at mid span on the left and right sides of the wheel and squeezing them together successively around the wheel. This action is sometimes accompanied by the sound of spokes untwisting in their nipples. This indicates that some spokes had a residual twist in them that should have been removed while truing the wheel. Stress-relieving is not intended to free the twist in the spokes. Spoke twist should be prevented by proper truing methods.

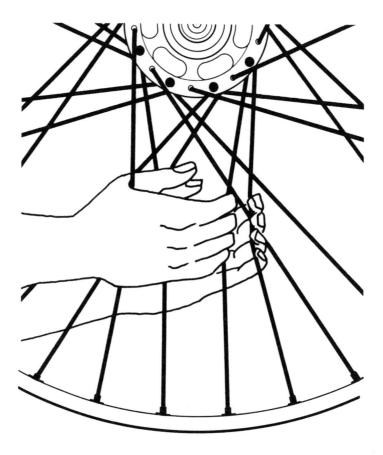

Fig. 35   Stress-relieving

Other methods of stress-relieving include placing the wheel on the floor and either walking on the spokes or pressing on the rim. With these methods the over-tensioning each spoke receives is difficult to control. Some spokes may be missed entirely and the one-sided load can damage the rim. Pressing on the rim is ineffective in stress-relieving because the applied force is distributed over too many spokes. This method is popular primarily because it releases spoke twist and makes reassuring clicks which are perceived to be beneficial.

TIED-AND-SOLDERED SPOKES

At the places where they are interlaced, spokes can be tied together with fine wire and then soldered. This procedure prevents broken spokes from tangling around the axle or derailleur. Extra strength has been attributed to tied-and-soldered wheels, but precise measurements and computations show that there is no change in lateral or torsional stiffness or strength (in small or large-flange wheels) between tied and untied spokes. The extremely small movement at the spoke crossings that tying restrains does not cause changes that can be measured by a micrometer. For radial loads there is even less theoretical room for motion. The only benefit of this procedure is restraint of broken spokes. Therefore, tying and soldering has little value especially for the track racing wheels that are most often tied.

Fig. 36   Tying and soldering

Part II

Building and Repairing Wheels

INTRODUCTION

The reasons for some wheel-building procedures may not be obvious at first. But with patience and understanding you can easily build good wheels. I will discuss methods for building and repairing wheels, the necessary tools, and some common problems. The theory upon which these methods are based is discussed in detail in the first part of the book. When in doubt, review the appropriate sections.

Note that illustrations of wheels use large-flange hubs for clarity and are not meant to imply that this is the preferred hub design.

PARTS AND TOOLS

A wheel is composed of a hub, a rim, spokes and nipples, components that should be selected to meet your requirements based on concepts discussed in PART I. Your only essential tool is a spoke wrench. Your bicycle is an adequate truing stand. The brake pads or a clothespin attached to the brake caliper can be used as a reference probe to measure wheel alignment.

When purchasing components, be prepared to choose from the following alternatives:

1. RIM: number of spokes, aluminum or steel, conventional or tubular, tire size, width, Schrader or Presta valve, and straight or hooked bead for clinchers

2. HUBS: flange size, number of spokes, aluminum or steel, quick release or plain axle, type of bearings

3. SPOKES: length, butted or straight, plated or stainless, thick or thin, length of nipples

Some of these choices are best resolved when you are able to compare components at the bicycle store. However, don't go to the store without being prepared to ask the right questions. Before leaving the store make sure that the number of holes in the hub(s) and rim(s) is correct; that the nipples fit the spoke threads; and that all the spokes are the correct type and length.

With hundreds of combinations of length and size that are indistinguishable unless measured, spokes often get mixed up at bicycle stores. Be wary of loose spokes and measure each one. To avoid errors, buy a sealed box of spokes even if there are a few more spokes than you need.

Achieving better cycling performance through more expensive components is mostly an illusion. However, you should expect to pay more for durable and reliable parts. Advice that certain rims, spokes or hubs will improve cycling performance should be taken with caution. Spend your money for hubs with better bearings and quick releases, durable spokes, and rims that fit your tire snugly and don't get fatigue cracks. Stay away from odd shaped rims with exotic coatings, non-round spokes, and aluminum nipples unless you can justify the expense and drawbacks that come with them.

HOW TO SELECT COMPONENTS

The following is a summary of criteria for selecting components. If you already have these items then skip to GETTING READY.

RIMS

Select a rim that fits the type and size of tires available in the region where you intend to ride. Some special tires are not universally distributed. Aluminum-alloy rims should have steel ferrules or washers to support the nipples. Verify that the rim is available for the same number of spokes as the hub.

HUBS

Aluminum-alloy hubs are better than steel ones because they are strong, yet soft enough so that spoke elbows can seat into the flanges. If steel hubs are used, they should have flanges thick enough to fully support the spoke elbows. Most steel hubs do not, so the spokes will bend and suffer early fatigue and failures. This effect can be reduced by modifying the spoke elbows as shown.

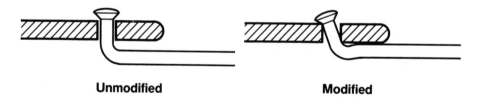

Unmodified   **Modified**

Fig. 37   Adjusting spokes to a thin flange

SPOKES

Unbutted spokes respond more quickly to adjustments than butted ones. However, they are more difficult to tension uniformly, and with non-uniform tension, looser spokes become slack in use and allow nipples to unscrew. Butted spokes are more elastic and distribute forces better in the rim. Butted spokes twist more while being tightened and respond less directly to truing corrections. A wheel with unbutted spokes will be easier to true but butted spokes will make a more durable wheel.

If a spoke distributor's reference table for lengths is not available, the correct spoke length can be calculated from equations in the back of the book. The length of a spoke is measured from the inside of the elbow to the end of the spoke. Choose a length that is within a millimeter of the correct length. This will ensure that no spoke will protrude from the nipples and puncture the tube. For tubular tires, exact length is not so important because spokes can protrude safely as much as three millimeters.

A spoke length correction can be made for offset rear wheels requiring spokes that are flush with the top of the nipple. Select the spokes for the left side one millimeter longer, and the rest one millimeter shorter, than the value calculated. The length correction is only approximate but for five- and six-speed wheels it is fairly accurate. Note that when tightened, spokes elongate and the rim shrinks, making the spokes effectively as much as a millimeter longer.

NIPPLES

It is best to use the same brand of nipples and spokes. If the manufacturer offers several lengths, use the shortest ones that still give adequate access for a spoke wrench. Note that, regardless of length, nipples generally have only about four millimeters of threads at the head end and a smooth bore for the remainder of their length.

SPOKE WRENCH

A specific spoke wrench is difficult to recommend because everyone has reasons for using a particular wrench. However, a good wrench should have hardened steel jaws, enough grip to afford good leverage, and should fit comfortably in the hand. It should fit the nipples closely. If its jaws are too wide, they will round the nipples. Some spoke wrenches are made for occasional repairs, others are for building wheels. The former are often found in repair kits, while the latter are usually sold separately in good bicycle shops.

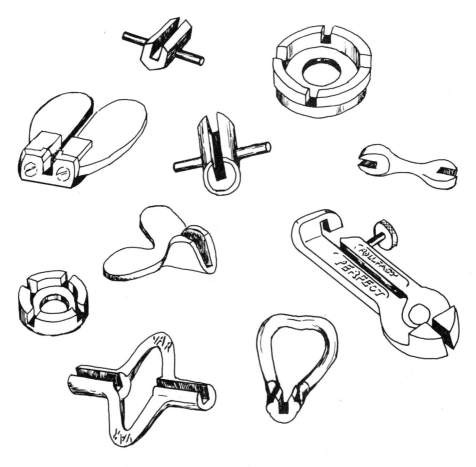

Fig. 38   Spoke wrenches

GETTING READY

Check the number of holes in the rim and hub, and check that you have enough spokes and nipples. Make sure that the spokes of each set are the same length within a millimeter. Arrange them with their heads at the same end. Tap the threaded ends against a table until they are even and weed out any odd-length spokes. Oil the threads of the whole bunch with motor oil or medium-weight machine oil. After wiping off the excess oil, place the spokes where they will be handy. Put the nipples in a bowl where you can pick them up easily. Prepare a comfortable seat in a well-lighted work area.

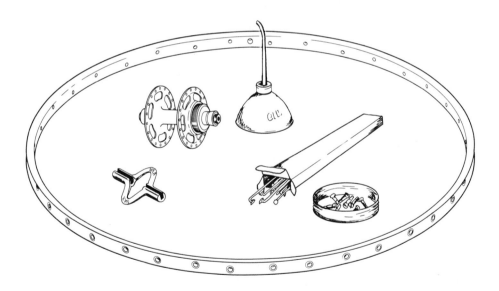

Fig. 39 Getting ready to build a wheel

INSERTING THE SPOKES

Each flange has an even number of holes. However, the holes in one flange are offset so that they are half way between the holes in the opposite flange, Look straight across the hub and you can see this offset. Half of the holes of each flange will be filled with spokes from the inside (spoke heads between the flanges), called outbound spokes, and half from outside the flanges, called inbound spokes. The inbound spokes are inserted first.

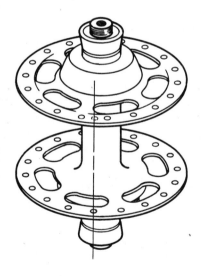

Fig. 40 Spoke hole offset in the hub

THE FIRST SPOKE

If this is a front wheel, skip to ALL HUBS. Since the rear hub transmits torque, its spokes have a preferred orientation that is described in PART I. To produce this orientation, the placement of the first spoke must be specially selected. Lay the rim on your lap with the valve stem hole opposite you. If the spoke hole on the right of the stem hole is lower than the one on the left, then hold the hub with its sprocket end down. Otherwise, hold the sprocket end up. If the holes lie exactly along the centerline of the rim, hold the sprocket end down.

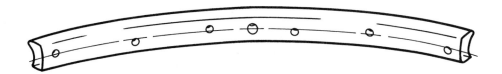

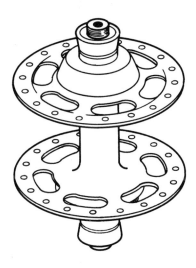

Fig. 41 Starting position for the rear hub

ALL HUBS

Hold the hub with its axle vertical, and drop an inbound spoke into every second hole of the upper flange, leaving an empty hole between each spoke. Put the rim on your lap with the valve stem hole opposite you, and notice that its holes are alternately offset up and down. Sometimes this offset is very slight and difficult to see. Put one of the inbound spokes into the hole that is next to the valve stem hole and offset upward. For rims having holes with no offset, put the first spoke to the left of the valve stem hole. Screw a nipple on it about four turns.

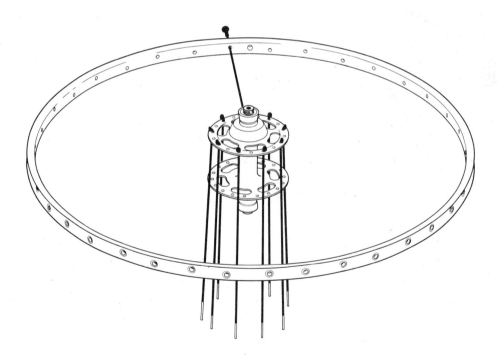

Fig. 42   Inserting the first spoke

THE FIRST SET

The remainder of the inbound spokes from this flange go into every fourth hole in the rim, leaving three empty holes between spokes. Make certain that all of these spokes go into holes that are offset upward. Thread nipples four turns onto each of these spokes.

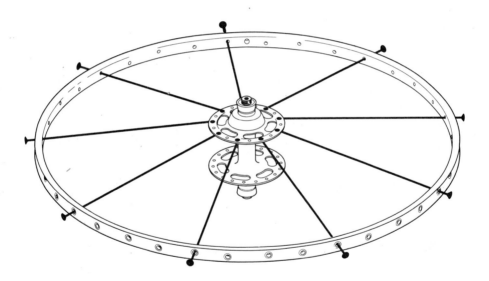

Fig. 43   The first set of spokes

THE SECOND SET

Turn the wheel over and prepare to insert the second set of inbound spokes. Select a hole in the rim that is next to the first spoke of the first set and one hole farther away from the valve stem hole. Next, carefully select a hole in the upper flange that lies next to the first spoke, and to the same side as the selected hole in the rim.

Remember that instead of lying directly opposite each other, the hole patterns in the flanges are offset a half space. To find the flange hole that lies on the correct side of the first spoke, insert a spoke through the upper flange, allowing it to butt into the other flange next to the first spoke. When this spoke is held parallel to the hub axle, you should be able to see whether it lies on the correct side of the first spoke of the first set. Install a spoke in the selected position and screw a nipple on about four turns. Now, put an inbound spoke into every second hole in this flange.

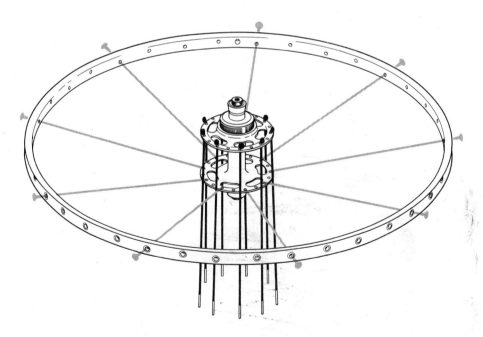

Fig. 44   The second set of spokes

Engage the remainder of these spokes in every fourth hole in the rim beginning with the spoke just installed. Rather than crossing each other, the two sets of spokes should lie nearly parallel. Screw a nipple on each spoke about four turns. Then check the spoke spacing in the rim and hub. The rim should have a regular pattern of two adjacent spokes and two empty holes. The hub should have a spoke in every second hole of its flanges and no spokes should cross others.

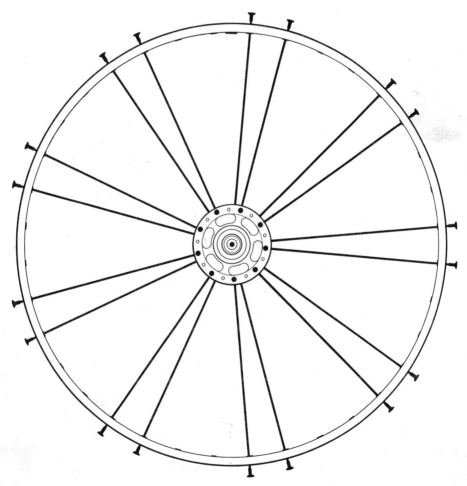

Fig. 45 Inbound spokes in place

THE THIRD SET

Without changing the position of the wheel, drop an outbound spoke into each of the remaining holes in the lower flange. Carefully turn the wheel over allowing the spokes to hang free while shaking the wheel gently so that the spokes fan out and lie parallel to the plane of the wheel. If the spokes fit tightly in the flange holes, you may have to force them to fan out properly.

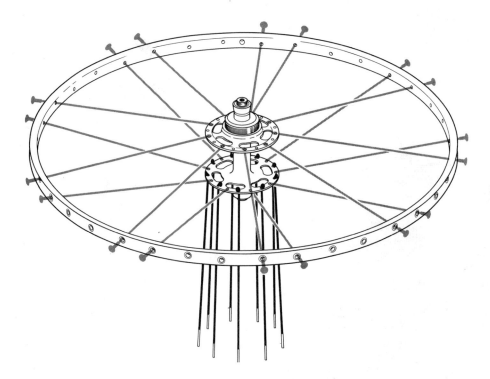

Fig. 46   The outbound spokes

CROSSING THE SPOKES

Twist the hub so that the first (inbound) spoke pulls away from the valve stem hole. Take one of the loose spokes and cross it over the number of adjacent inbound spokes required by the cross pattern. Cross it over the first spokes and under the last. This spoke goes into the first empty hole in the rim beyond the last spoke crossed. At first it may seem too short to reach this hole. If the hub is rotated properly with the nipples seated in the rim, and with spokes of the correct length, it will reach easily. Cross lace the rest of these spokes in the same manner.

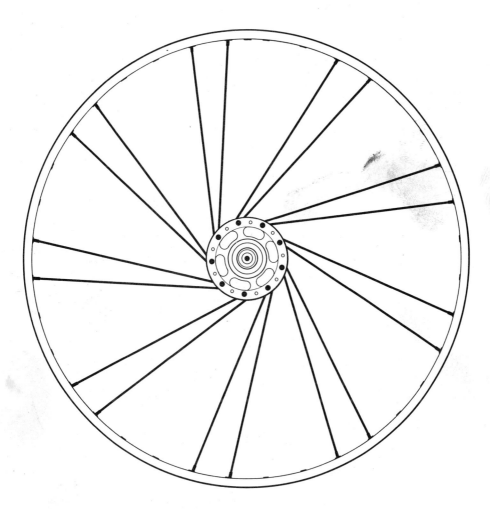

Fig. 47 Twisting the hub

If twisting the hub is difficult, then all nipples may not have dropped into their holes in the rim. Seating the nipples in rims with loose washers requires particular care. While winding up the hub, rotate the spokes in the flanges and make them more tangent to the hub. If the nipples were screwed on more than a few turns, the hub cannot twist properly. If the spoke still cannot engage the nipple, either the number of crosses is incorrect or the spokes are too short.

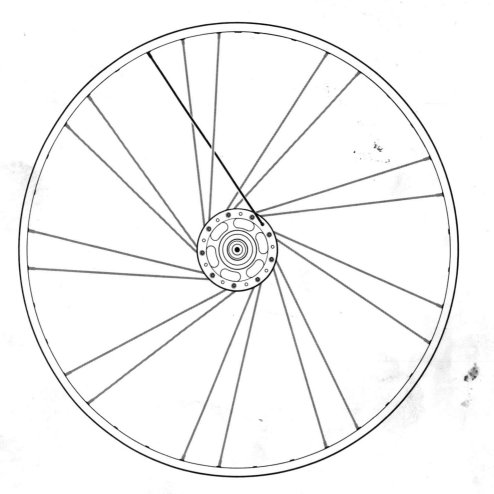

Fig. 48   Crossing the spokes

THE FOURTH SET

Insert the last set of outbound spokes into the remaining empty holes in the lower flange, then turn the wheel over and proceed as before. When all the spokes are in place, but still very loose, the following check of the spoke positions should be made:

1. The valve stem hole should lie between two nearly parallel spokes, leaving space for the tire pump.

2. All spokes should enter holes in the rim, offset toward their respective flanges.

3. All spokes should be uniformly loose. If any spokes are alternately tight and loose in pairs, then they are probably in the wrong holes in the hub or rim.

Errors in spoke placement must be corrected or the hub will be damaged when the spokes are tightened.

ALL THE SPOKES ARE IN

Now that the wheel is assembled it must be checked for correctness. Drive the outer spoke crossings toward the hub using a screwdriver handle between crossed pairs. Now the wheel should have a completely uniform spoke pattern. Each pair of crossed spokes from the same flange should occupy every second hole in the rim. All of the outer spoke crossings should lie at about the same radius from the hub.

Up to this point the assembly proceeded step-by-step in a fixed sequence. Although tensioning and truing the wheel are described in much the same manner, the phases of truing are not independent. Each adjustment will affect more than one aspect of alignment. Therefore, gradually combining lateral and radial adjustments will shorten the repetitive truing process. Consider both centering and tension while making the wheel laterally and radially true.

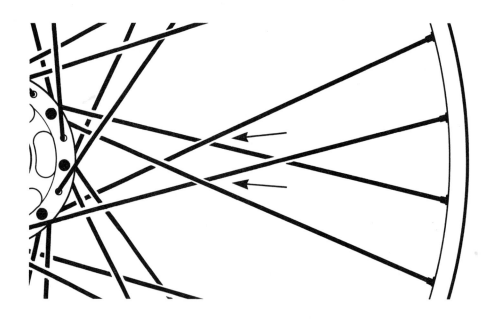

Fig. 49   Aligning the spokes

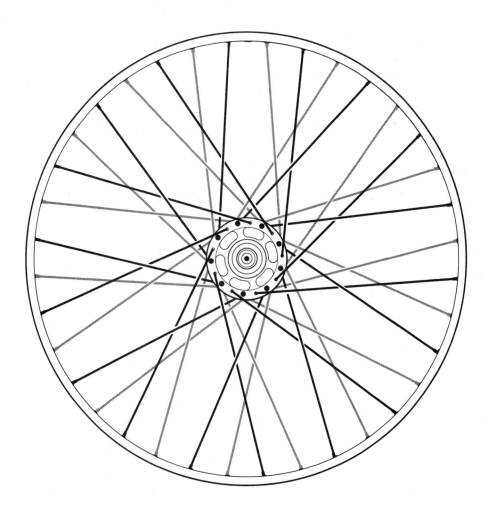

Fig. 50   The completely laced wheel

TENSIONING THE WHEEL

Wheel roundness is dependent on equal thread engagement for all spokes. While the spokes are still loose, they should all be adjusted to the same thread engagement. Later, when the wheel is tight, roundness is more difficult to correct. For convenience, always turn the spoke nipples so the wrench flats are parallel to the rim. With this method even a quarter turn is easily seen, and the spoke wrench can be readily engaged without fumbling. A quarter turn is a sufficiently fine adjustment for the smallest corrections.

WARNING
Tensioning spokes can be dangerous. A spoke that ruptures under tension can be shot from the rim into your eye, like an arrow from a crossbow. Never face directly into the line of the spokes while working on the wheel.

TAKING OUT THE SLACK
Using a spoke wrench or screwdriver, tighten all the nipples until two threads remain exposed where the spoke enters the nipple. Long nipples made for very thick rims should be advanced until the spokes are ready to emerge from the end of the nipple, and then backed out four turns. Position all nipples accurately to ensure that the wheel will be nearly true before tensioning. If the spokes become very tight during this process, they are too short. If the spokes are still very loose, tighten the nipples two more full turns. If the spokes are still slack by the time they emerge from the heads of the nipples, they are too long.

MAKING THEM TIGHT
Now the spokes are ready to be tensioned. Put the wheel in the truing fixture and, starting at the valve stem hole, tighten each spoke one turn. For rear wheels, (unless compensation for offset has been made by using spokes of unequal length) tension the spokes by first tightening only the spokes on the sprocket side three turns, one turn at a time. Continue to tighten only the spokes on the sprocket side (in quarter turns) until the wheel is roughly centered as described in the section on centering. If the rim was nearly true at the start, by tightening all the spokes equally it will stay that way.

Always start a round of adjustments at the stem hole so that you can tell when you are back at the start. After each complete round of tightening, check the tone of the wheel. If the spokes are tight enough to give a tone when plucked, then the wheel is ready to be trued. Note that some rims require the spokes adjacent to the joint to be one or more turns looser to correct for the thickness of the rim splice.

TENSION BY TONE

Throughout the following sections, tone is used to determine tension. The tone of a tight wheel is not easily described. It is best to compare the wheel you are building with one that is properly tight. If you cannot distinguish the tone of a correctly tensioned wheel, you can compare the feel of a good wheel by grasping and squeezing pairs of parallel spokes at mid span. If a comparison is not possible then stress-relieving should be used as a measure of maximum tension.

IMPROVING THE SPOKE LINE

If the spokes have a good snug fit in the flange, they will have a slight bow at the edge of the flange. The outbound spokes will bow out at the the flange. Press these spokes down near their elbows with your thumb so that they lie against the flange. A rubber or plastic mallet may be used, but only with great care. Inbound spokes usually lie flat and present no problem. These adjustments require skill that come with practice. Most hubs have their flanges angled inward slightly to reduce the difference between elbow bends of inbound and outbound spokes.

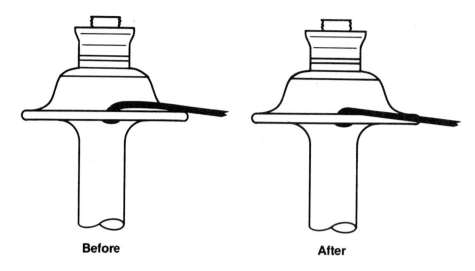

Before   **After**

Fig. 51   Improving the spoke line at the hub

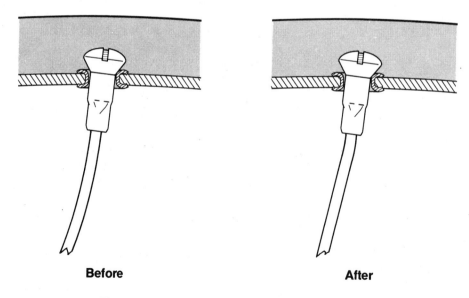

Before   **After**

Fig. 52   Improving the spoke line at the rim

Although the nipples swivel in the rim, with large flange hubs the spoke angle may be greater than this swivel allows. These spokes will curve on entering the nipple and the spoke will flex when the wheel is ridden, causing fatigue and premature failure. The desired spoke alignment is an abrupt bend as the spoke enters the nipple. This bend can be made with smooth-jawed pliers or by grasping pairs of crossing spokes near the rim and squeezing them firmly. This procedure, which should not be confused with stress relieving, is most effective when the wheel is moderately tensioned.

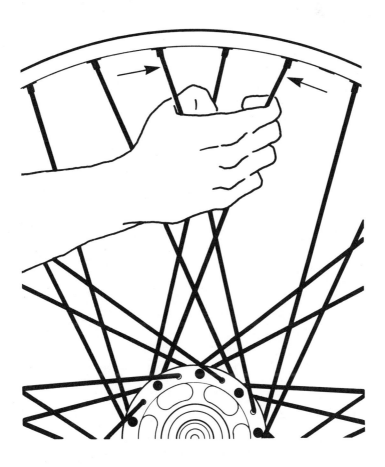

Fig. 53 Manually improving the spoke line

TRUING THE WHEEL

Wheel truing is a repetitive process by which spoke tension is gradually increased while alignment and centering are improved. Since the wheel is a pre-stressed elastic structure, changing tension in one spoke will cause tension changes in others. Be prepared to find alignment changes at places other than where the last adjustment was made. To make the nipples turn freely, apply a drop of oil to each spoke hole at the point where the nipple leaves the rim. Check hub bearings for play. Loose bearings cause random wobbles that are unaffected by truing.

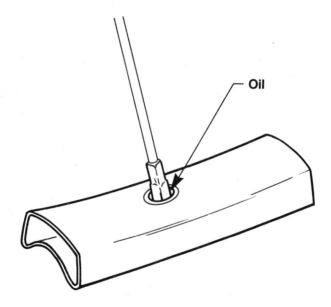

Fig. 54   Oiling the nipple sockets

SMALL AND LARGE ERRORS

The size of alignment errors depends on whether they are radial or lateral. Small lateral errors are one-half millimeter or less. Correcting these errors require only a quarter turn tighter and a quarter turn looser on opposing spokes. Very small errors require as little as a quarter turn on one side of the wheel only. Corrections of this magnitude also apply to centering (which is described later). For radial alignment, a half-millimeter change requires as much as two spoke threads and therefore two whole turns of the spoke nipple. Because the rim moves the same distance as the advance of the nipple, radial adjustments need be no finer than a half turn.

FIVE-, SIX-, AND SEVEN-SPEED WHEELS

Wheels with a large offset present special problems to the builder. Unlike front wheels they have large differences between the angles of the left and right spokes which make them respond differently to adjustments. Since the right side spokes are almost in the plane of the rim, adjusting them has little effect on lateral alignment. The spokes on the left, in contrast, pull to the side at a much broader angle and have a smaller effect on radial alignment. Wheels with a large offset must be trued taking these differences into consideration.

The tension ratios and, therefore, lateral adjustment ratios for different offsets are approximately: five-speed 1.6 to 1, six-speed 2 to 1, seven-speed 2.5 to 1. This means that for a radial adjustment on a six-speed wheel the right hand spokes must receive twice as many turns as every turn on the left to keep the wheel centered. However, for radial adjustments the right- and left-hand spokes take nearly the same adjustment to keep the wheel round. These changes are related to the sine and cosine of the lateral spoke angles. For these small angles the sine has a large effect while the cosine effect is nearly zero. It is usually simpler to ignore all this and correctly center the wheel in a separate step.

RADIAL TRUING

The aim of radial truing is to make the rim circular. Achieving radial alignment is difficult because it is hard to see whether there are more low or high spots on the rim. If lateral error is so great that radial errors are difficult to observe, work on lateral alignment first. If, however, both radial and lateral trueness are very poor, work on the worst of each until the alignment is good enough to allow a systematic approach.

Adjust the reference probe on the truing fixture so that it almost touches the outside of the rim as it turns. Consider the zones where the rim touches the probe as too high. Spokes in these zones must be tightened.

Locate the low zones and adjust their spokes by loosening them. Low zones cannot be corrected if the wheel is not tight enough because the rim will not respond unless there is tension in the spokes. Therefore, during the early adjustments, always tighten high spots first.

Check the relative tension of the spokes by plucking them at the nipple. A lower tone indicates lower tension. If a loose spoke lies in the center of a tight zone, or a tight spoke lies in the center of a loose zone, adjust only the odd spoke to make the correction. Note that a rear wheel with an offset hub will have different tensions on the left and right sides. The spokes of each side should be uniformly tight among themselves.

When a full turn does not correct an alignment error, do not continue to adjust at the same place. Rotate the wheel and gradually correct the worst errors first. To avoid large differences in tension among spokes,

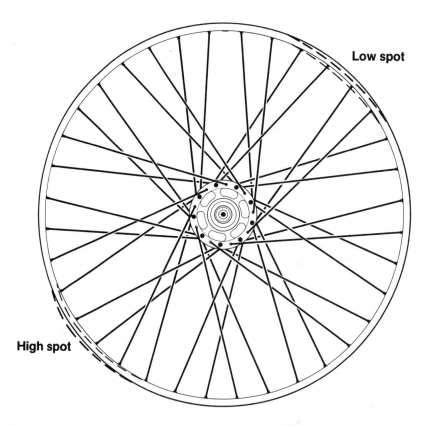

Fig. 55 Radial alignment

always make the largest correction in the center of an error, decreasing to a quarter turn at the ends. Be careful to keep spoke tension low until the last pass through the truing process. If tension seems prematurely high, loosen all spokes a half turn before continuing. Excessive tension during truing may damage the threads or flat faces of the nipples.

LATERAL TRUING

Lateral truing aligns the rim so that it lies in a plane (makes it flat). If the wheel is grossly out-of-round, errors in lateral alignment are difficult to see, so work on radial alignment first. To improve lateral alignment, adjust the reference probe on the truing fixture so that it comes close to, but does not touch, the side of the rotating wheel. Visually estimate the average position of the rim with respect to the probe. This is the average of wobbles to the left and right based on both their number and size. Loosen and tighten opposing spokes (spokes coming from the opposite side of the hub) equally to move the rim toward this position.

Check the relative tension of the spokes by plucking them at the nipple. Remember that a lower tone indicates lower tension. As in radial truing, if a loose or a tight spoke lies in the center of the wobble, adjust only the odd spoke to make the correction. Note that a rear wheel with an offset hub will have a different tension on the left and right side. The spokes of each side should be uniformly tight among themselves.

To correct a lateral error, tighten the spokes from one flange and loosen the ones from the opposite flange in that zone. If the wobble is to the right, the spokes on the right must be loosened and those on the left tightened. The amount depends on the size of the error and the type of spokes and hub. However, do not exceed one turn unless you are tightening a very loose spoke. Adjust the spokes in the middle of the wobble most, and those on the ends a quarter turn. Tighten and loosen opposing spokes equally. By just tightening or just loosening, the lateral alignment may improve, but radial trueness will suffer. However, with offset wheels the spoke response-to-correction ratios mentioned for five-, six-, and seven-speed wheels should be considered.

CENTERING

As the wheel nears completion, it must be made symmetric so that the rear wheel will lie directly behind the front wheel and the bicycle will ride with proper balance. The rim of a correctly centered wheel lies midway between the faces of the axle lock nuts. Wheel symmetry can be measured by reversing the wheel in the fixture. This will show twice the lateral position error from the reference probe. A fixture with built-

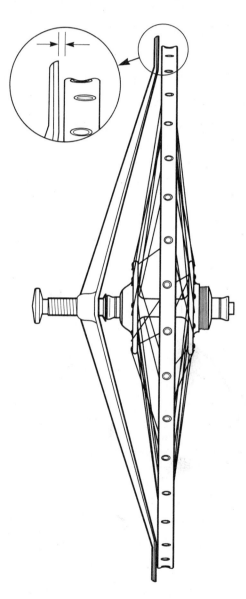

Fig. 56 Centering the wheel

in centering (probes on both sides) can save the process of reversing the wheel, but a centering tool generally gives the most precise measurement. Centering measurements show whether the axle protrudes more from one side of the rim centerline than the other. Tighten the spokes on the side where the axle extends farther.

When centering, as with the other alignment procedures, always begin at the valve stem hole and proceed around the wheel to ensure that no spokes are missed or adjusted twice. Make corrections by tightening the spokes that pull the rim toward the center and loosening those that will allow it to move that direction. To increase tension while centering, make corrections by tightening only. However, if this is an early correction, or if tension already is high enough, alternately loosen and tighten opposing spokes equally to maintain tension. A half turn will be enough for larger errors, a quarter turn for smaller ones. Finally, for fine adjustments, take a quarter turn on one side only, or even a quarter turn on every second spoke on one side.

THE RIM JOINT

Most rims are made from straight material that is formed into a hoop and joined by welding or splicing. The joint often causes irregular alignment that is difficult to correct. For spliced rims, the extent of the error may not appear until after the spokes are tensioned. In both welded and spliced rims spoke tension may not be uniform near the joint. However, completely correcting this error may be impossible. Straightening the rim by the methods described under soft failures can achieve a better balance of spoke tension.

FINAL TENSIONING

At this stage the wheel should be radially and laterally true and centered, but not fully tensioned. To achieve maximum strength, tension the spokes near the maximum that the rim permits. Spoke tension can be measured directly with a tensiometer but it also can be determined by comparing the tone of the wheel to another properly-tensioned wheel of the same type. For the best ring, pluck the spokes at the nipples. By matching the tones of the spokes they can be brought very close to the same tension. If the rim was initially straight, all spokes on each side of the wheel should have the same tension. For offset rear wheels, the spokes on the gear cluster side should have a uniformly higher tone than the others.

Non-uniform tension indicates an imbalance that will eventually cause misalignment.

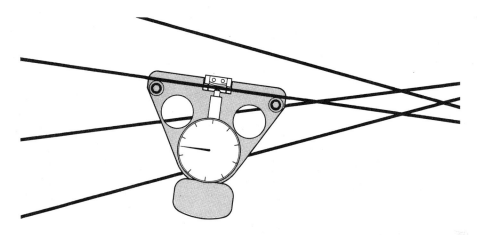

Fig. 57   Measuring tension

WIND-UP

As they are tightened, spokes twist from friction and thread slope. To relieve twist, overtighten spokes a quarter turn with each adjustment and then back off a quarter turn. Butted spokes require more overshoot than unbutted spokes. With experience sensing the amount of wind-up becomes a matter of touch. Overtighten just enough so that no twist remains when the nipple is backed off. At the point where no twist remains, the torque required to tighten and loosen the spoke is equal.

FINDING THE RIGHT TENSION

Increase tension by tightening each spoke a quarter turn starting at the valve stem hole. After each round, test the tension by stress-relieving. The maximum safe tension is exceeded when the wheel becomes untrue during stress relieving. Ideal tension should be approached carefully to avoid rim damage. When the wheel loses alignment from stress-relieving, loosen all spokes a half turn and re-true the wheel. Stress-relieving, which is discussed in a following section, increases tension enough to overload the rim if the spokes are too tight. A strong and safe wheel should be able to withstand about a ten percent overload without damage. Note that tightening all the spokes of an offset rear wheel will move the rim away from the sprocket side as described in the section FIVE-, SIX-, AND SEVEN-SPEED WHEELS. Now check the radial and lateral alignment and centering again. Only very small changes, if any, should be required.

BALANCING TENSION

Although the wheel now may be true, it should be fine-tuned to ensure that it will remain that way. If the spokes are not equally tight now they will equalize in use and the wheel will lose alignment. Listen to the tone of each spoke to find which ones are tighter and which ones are looser. On rear wheels the right side should be tighter than the left. Correct for a tight spoke by loosening it and tightening its neighbors (on the same side of the wheel) so that alignment remains unchanged. For example, if only one spoke is a half turn too tight, loosen it and tighten its neighbors a quarter turn each. Use the reverse method for loose spokes. Rim imperfections such as the rim joint make achieving complete uniformity impossible without losing alignment. After balancing tension as well as possible, true the wheel where necessary.

STRESS-RELIEVING

Although stress-relieving is often omitted, it is one of the most important operations in wheel building. Failure to stress-relieve is the most common cause of early spoke failures. A detailed analysis of this process appears in PART I.

To stress-relieve, grasp the most nearly parallel pairs of spokes at mid span on both sides of the wheel. The hands should be nearly palm-to-palm. Squeeze the spoke pairs vigorously. Wear leather-faced gloves for hand protection. Repeat this process, squeezing opposing pairs until all spokes have been squeezed. If after stress-relieving the wheel is appreciably out of true in four big smooth waves, then it was over-tensioned and re-truing should begin by relaxing tension about a half-turn all around. Usually, only small lateral corrections are required after stress relieving.

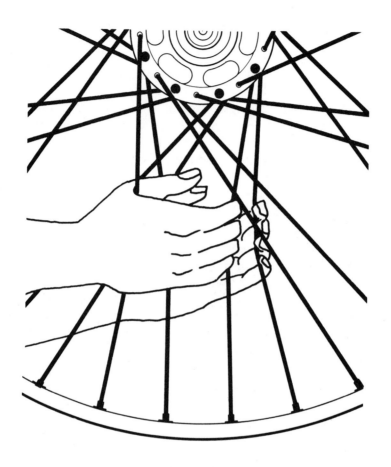

Fig. 58 Stress-relieving

THE WHEEL IS FINISHED

When the wheel is stress-relieved and has had final truing, it is finished and ready to use. The following sections treat optional features that apply in special cases.

TYING AND SOLDERING

The spokes of wheels used for racing are sometimes secured by tying and soldering. The interlaced spoke crossings are wrapped with fine wire to hold them firmly together. Wrap fine (about 0.5 mm) pre-tinned copper wire one layer thick over about three millimeters of the crossing. After completing all the ties, solder them (with rosin core solder for zinc or cadmium plated spokes, and acid core for stainless, nickel, or chrome-plated spokes) so that the solder wets both the wire and spokes. This requires a high temperature soldering iron. Never use a flame, because this can easily overheat and damage the spokes. Remove residual acid flux with hot water and soap or baking soda.

Fig. 59 Tying and soldering

OTHER SPOKE PATTERNS

Spoke patterns other than cross lacing are possible. The merits of these are discussed in PART I. Radial spoking is described here because it is the only other pattern commonly used. Hubs with keyhole-shaped spoke holes are also treated.

RADIAL SPOKING

Flange stresses at the spoke holes of a radially-spoked wheel are higher than for any other spoke pattern. These stresses often lead to flange failure for aluminum-alloy hubs. For this reason radial spoking is not recommended. Since radial spoking requires no special starting point and has no preferred sequence of spoke insertion, it is relatively simple.

Hold the hub with one end up and drop a spoke into every hole of the lower flange. With the rim on your lap, insert these spokes into alternate rim holes that are offset downward. Screw a nipple onto each spoke about four turns. Turn the wheel over and insert the remaining spokes in the same manner. Radial spokes can be laced either all inbound or all outbound or alternating. However, all outbound spokes give the widest effective flange spacing and inbound spokes give lowest stress. Truing is the same as for tangential spokes.

KEY HOLED HUBS

Some hubs are made with keyhole-shaped spoke holes. With this design, spokes can be inserted head first and need not be threaded through the holes in the flanges. Although keyholes give poorer spoke support than closely fitting holes, they are necessary when one flange is much larger than the other. Hub brakes and generator hubs often have a small flange with keyholes. Spoke these hubs the same as an ordinary hub if both sides of the wheel are to have the same cross pattern. Wooden matchsticks or small pieces of rubber tubing can be used to plug the keyholes and keep the first spokes from falling out of the hub while inserting the others. Thread the nipples onto the spokes before hooking the spokes into the keyholes.

If the flange diameters are different, use a fully tangential pattern on the small flange and lace the large flange crossed one or two. This gives in nearly equal spoke angles at the rim, and makes a more aesthetically pleasing wheel than one with identically crossed spokes. Wheels with two spoke patterns are best spoked one side at a time since each pattern requires an independent assembly.

MIXED SPOKE PATTERNS

Sometimes a hub requires two different spoke patterns or you decide to build such a wheel by choice. Although these wheels are best laced one side at a time, this method has two principal disadvantages. First, the inbound spokes of the second side must be fed through the crossed spokes of the first side and, second, the location of the spokes in the second set is difficult to describe.

SPOKING ONE SIDE AT A TIME

Follow the general method for spoking wheels (previously described) through the point where the first set of inbound spokes is engaged in the rim. After the first set of inbound spokes is in place, turn the wheel over and insert a spoke in each remaining hole in the same flange. Turn the wheel over and fan the spokes so that they lie parallel to the plane of the wheel. Twist the hub so that the inbound spokes pull away from the valve stem hole. Cross any loose spoke over the number of adjacent inbound spokes required by the selected cross pattern. Cross it over the first ones and under the last one. This spoke goes into the second empty hole in the rim beyond the last spoke crossed. At first it may seem too short to reach this hole, but if the hub is rotated properly and the nipples are seated in the rim, the spoke will fit easily.

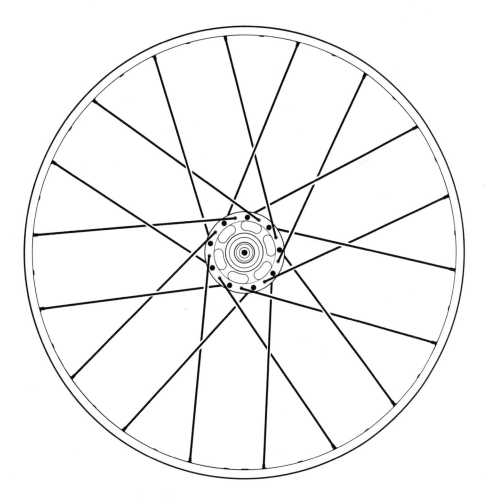

Fig. 60   Crossing the spokes

The second side of the hub can be laced in the same or a different pattern. In either case the inbound spokes will go into holes in the hub that are a half space farther away from and to the same side of the valve stem hole as the first spoke. If the same cross pattern is used, then one of these inbound spokes should lie nearly parallel to the first spoke, and one hole in the rim farther away from the valve stem hole. The method for placing this first inbound spoke of the second side is described in the general section on lacing spokes. If this side is to be crossed one

less than the first side, this spoke goes into the rim one empty hole farther away from the stem hole than if the patterns were the same on both
sides. For each crossing less, add one empty hole; for each crossing more,
subtract one empty hole.

The inbound spokes of the second side can be passed between the loose
spoke crossings of the other side. This requires bending them only slightly. After placing the first inbound spoke of the second side and threading

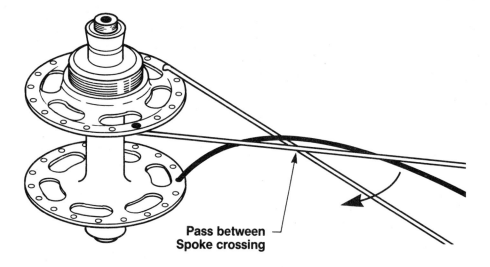

**Pass between
Spoke crossing**

Fig. 61   Threading spokes through crossed spokes

a nipple on it, insert the rest of the inbound spokes in every second
hole in the hub and their proper hole in the rim. Check that the remaining empty rim holes are equally spaced. Hold the wheel so that
the empty holes are in the lower flange and drop a spoke into each empty
hole. Turn the wheel over and fan the spokes so that they lie parallel
to the plane of the wheel. Cross any loose spoke over as many adjacent
inbound spokes as the selected cross pattern requires. Cross it over the
first ones and under the last one. Engage the remaining spokes in the
rim, and screw a nipple on each about four turns. Now true the wheel
as described in the general truing section.

WHEEL REPAIR

Many damaged wheels can be repaired. A broken spoke, the most common failure, is the easiest to repair. Rim damage is usually more difficult to fix, and sometimes even the best of craftsmen cannot true a bent rim even though the bend is smooth.

SPOKE FAILURE

When a spoke fails from fatigue there is usually no rim damage. However, if the spoke was forcefully broken, there may be a visible bend in the rim. Such a bend, if it spans fewer than four spokes, is called a kink and may need straightening. If there is no kink, a new spoke can be inserted and tightened to the tension of its neighbors. If this does not re-true the wheel, lay the wheel on the floor with the new spoke on the upper side and the rim touching the floor at the new spoke. Press down on the rim about four spokes to either side of the new spoke. Forcing the rim like this will help the new spoke restore rim alignment. Use this method only if the rim misalignment is less than about ten millimeters; otherwise treat the damage as a soft wheel failure, which is described in the following section.

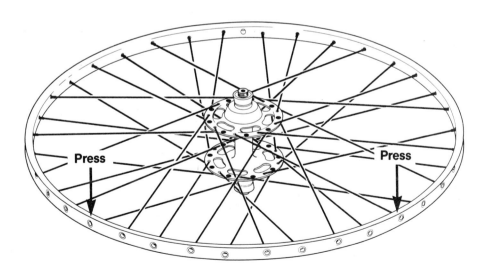

Fig. 62 Straightening the rim

Correct the spoke line of the new spoke and stress-relieve the whole wheel as previously described. Stress-relieving may break other fatigue-damaged spokes. Finally, true the wheel in the conventional manner. If the new spoke has higher-than-average tension, repeat the process of pressing the rim against the floor.

SOFT WHEEL FAILURE

In a soft failure the rim has a smooth bend and only a few spokes are loose. If the wheel is deformed laterally more than ten millimeters, all spokes should be loosened about two turns before attempting to straighten the wheel. Attempting to straighten the rim by bending it with the spokes in their original adjustment would, in effect, straighten and tension the wheel at the same time. Straightening makes the rim material yield and take a new set. When the rim yields, it deforms not only in response to the straightening forces, but also to the spoke forces. These combined forces will cause kinks in the rim at each spoke.

To repair a soft failure begin by loosening all spokes about two turns, even those that are no longer tight. Lay the wheel on its side and press down on the rim adjacent to the low parts, turning the wheel over if necessary, until the rim is reasonably straight. Place the wheel in the truing fixture and begin tensioning and aligning. If the misalignment is still more than ten millimeters, repeat the procedure on the floor as tension increases. Now true the wheel as previously described. Because straightened rims usually have non-uniform spoke tension, the wheel will probably not stay true.

DENTED RIM

Although some dents can be repaired satisfactorily this procedure is generally used only to make a wheel usable until a new rim can be obtained. As with the soft failure, this repair makes the rim material yield. If the wheel is tensioned while it yields, further damage will occur from the combination of spoke tension and straightening forces. Therefore, relax spoke tension before straightening the rim. If the rim curves radially inward at or near a spoke, remove this spoke before straightening and use shaped piece of wood and hammer to straighten the indentation. Specially-shaped pliers are available to re-shape some rims. After repairing the dent proceed as with soft failures.

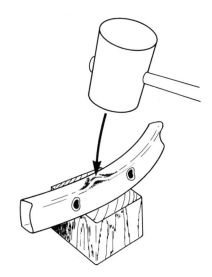

Fig. 63   Repairing a dented rim

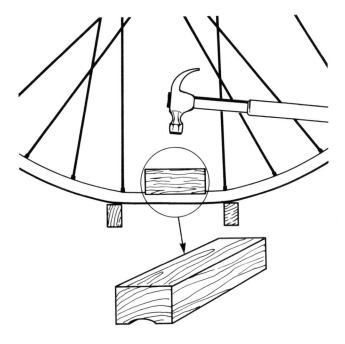

Fig. 64   Repairing a radial dent

REPLACING A RIM

When the rim of a good wheel is damaged beyond repair but the spokes have no kinks, the wheel can be rebuilt more easily than starting from scratch. If the wheel is still somewhat round, and no spokes are broken, the spokes can be transferred from the damaged rim to a new one. Lay the new rim on top of the old one so that the valve stem holes are side-by-side. Make sure that the spoke holes in both rims are offset to the same side. Unscrew the nipples one-at-a-time and transfer the spokes to the new rim. Only spokes that cannot be straightened by hand need be replaced. Lubricate the spoke threads before re-installing and replace nipples that have deformed flanks. After all spokes have been transferred, follow the procedure for truing a new wheel.

REUSED SPOKES

If a wheel is destroyed in a crash, spokes are seldom broken unless some obstacle got between them. These spokes are as good as before the crash and can be reused in a new wheel. Because the wheel was pre-stressed, none of the spokes was over-stressed in the crash. Only the rim was damaged, not the spokes. However, the spokes should not be removed from the hub. They should be reused as described in "REPLACING A RIM." Because they have been stress-relieved and have acquired a unique form, they will not fit properly in new positions in a different wheel. By coincidence some may do well if reused, but the probability of a number of mismatches makes reuse after unspoking a bad practice.

If you have a rim replaced in a bicycle shop, the store will usually insist that all spokes be replaced as well. The mechanic will not want you to gauge the quality of his work on possible failures of your used spokes, whose condition cannot be determined by inspection.

OPTIONAL TOOLS AND THEIR USES

Few tools are required to build good wheels. In fact a bicycle and a spoke wrench are adequate equipment. However, a few other items described in the following sections can increase the speed and convenience of building and truing wheels.

TRUING STAND

A bicycle can be used as a truing stand. Use the brake as the gauge point against which to measure misalignment by adjusting the brake caliper so that the pad is close to the rim. Some builders prefer to use their thumb as a gauge even when using a well-equipped stand. The best truing stands have fast wheel mounting, a quickly adjustable gauge point and adjustment for different hub widths and wheel sizes, and they are rigid. In addition, some deluxe versions may have automatic centering, dial gauges for measuring radial and lateral alignment, lights, rim straighteners and other features.

Although the precision of dial gauges exceeds the requirements of wheel truing, they have their merits. By recording dial reading at each spoke, a graph of the alignment can be made. For each spoke, move to the right five millimeters on the graph and for each tenth of a millimeter deflection, move up or down a millimeter. A straight line through this plot shows which spokes are too loose and which are too tight. That is, the proper position of the rim can be determined, and high and low spots (left and right) adjusted accordingly. Since the wheel is an elastic structure, changing any one of the spokes causes some change in others. So either with or without dial gauges, truing is a repetitive process.

CENTERING TOOL

Properly built front and rear wheels are centered between their axle lock nuts. A wheel may be centered during the truing process by reversing it in the truing fixture. If the rim is not in the same location after reversal, the wheel is not centered. To correct centering errors, spokes on one side of the wheel are tightened and the others loosened.

A centering tool allows quick and precise measurement of how well a wheel is centered. The tool consists of a bridge that spans the diameter of the wheel with a probe to locate the axle lock nut. It measures which end of the axle protrudes farther from the rim center line. The bridge is placed on the rim while the probe is advanced until it just makes contact with the axle lock nut. Then it is placed on the opposite side of the wheel. When one end of the bridge is pressed against the rim the space at the other end represents four times the centering error. The centering tool magnifies the error because it shows the sum of two differential measurements.

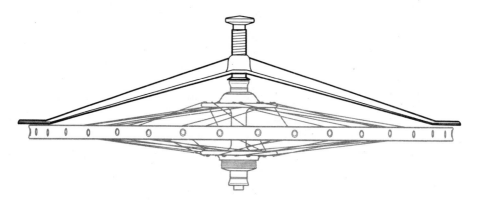

Fig. 65   Centering tool

NIPPLE DRIVER

A special spoke nipple screwdriver with a pilot pin in the center of the blade simplifies bringing all the spokes to the same thread engagement. The pilot pin fits into the nipple so that as the spoke advances in the threads, it ejects the screwdriver at the desired thread engagement. This type of blade is often used with a push-type (Yankee) screwdriver or a crank handle. Of these, the crank-handle type is much faster and easier to use.

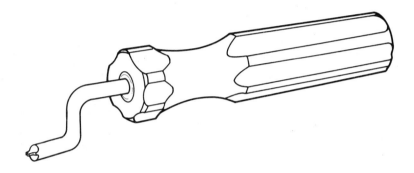

Fig. 66   Nipple driver

TENSIOMETER

Most wheels are built by feel, and their final tension is strongly influenced by the mood of the builder. A tension measuring tool is useful for repeatably building tight wheels. Such a tool, a tensiometer, measures the deflection of the spoke under a standard load over a given span. The dial is calibrated in tension or deflection. Either measure is equally useful for wheel building. It is not important to determine the exact tension but rather that the wheel is up to the desired mark. The correct maximum for a specific wheel design must still be determined first by stress-relieving. For subsequent wheels the tensiometer can be used to accurately and quickly bring the wheel to the desired tension.

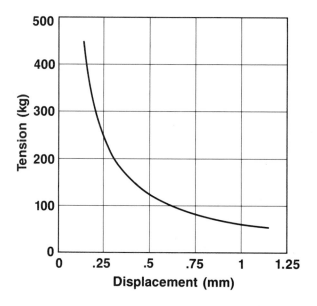

$$T = \frac{Force}{2\,TAN\,\theta} = \frac{Force \times L}{2\,D}$$

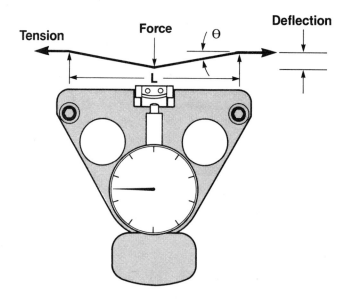

Fig. 67   Tensiometer

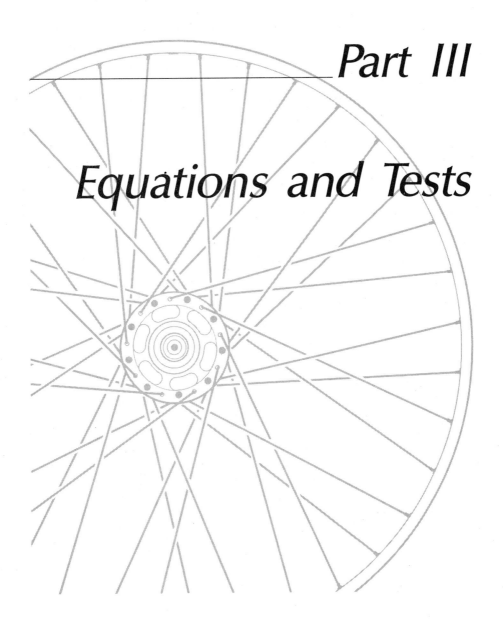

Part III

Equations and Tests

INTRODUCTION

Measurements were made to confirm the values indicated by theory and to substantiate that the correct theory was applied. Tensile tests of various brands and types of spokes were performed to determine the elastic limits, ultimate strengths and ductilities. The fatigue resistance of spokes was not tested for lack of suitable equipment. Wheels were tested for distribution of vertical loads. Stiffness and strength under lateral and torsional loads were measured before and after tying and soldering.

TYING AND SOLDERING

A low- and high-flange rear wheel were each tested for lateral and tor-sional elasticity. The hub of the wheel being tested was securely held in a machine tool vise by means of a modified freewheel core. A dial gauge was mounted on the machine bed to record deflections. The lateral deflection caused by a 16 kg weight applied at four separate locations was repeatable and unchanged at these locations within 0.05 mm before and after the spokes were tied. The torsional deflection was also measured on the same fixture.

For the torsional test a steel wire was wrapped around the rim and an-chored in the valve stem hole. A force of 30 kg on the wire produced a rotational movement of 1.65 mm on a large flange 36 butted spoke wheel, and 3.43 mm on a similar small flange wheel. The measurements were repeated several times and averaged, both before and after tying. The results in each case showed a change of about 2% which was also the variance of the measurements that were averaged. For the small flange wheel the deflection decreased when tied, while for the large flange wheel it increased. It is apparent from these results that tying and solder-ing of spokes has so little effect, if any, that it is difficult to detect even by precise measurement.

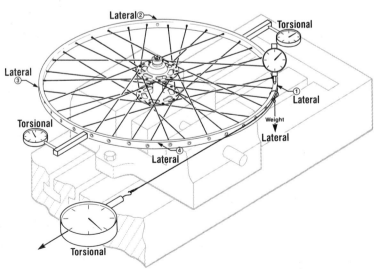

Fig. 68 Lateral and torsional strength

SPOKE STRENGTH

Butted and unbutted spokes in 2.0 and 1.8 mm diameters of two typical high quality brands were tested in a tensile testing machine for ultimate strength and ductility. In contrast to tests performed for the first edition of this book, these spokes withstood substantial elongation before failure. Some butted spokes stretched more than six millimeters without breaking, at which point the test was stopped. Butted spokes failed in their reduced diameter mid-sections while the unbutted spokes failed at their elbows.

For the test, spokes were anchored between an aluminum plate similar to the flange of a high quality hub and a standard threaded nipple. Sets of three spokes of each kind were tested and each set produced uniform results. The curves shown show the average response of each set. The results show that there is little measurable difference in strength among these spokes and suggest that their differences, if any, lie in fatigue characteristics that depend on their alloy, temper, butting, and how they are built into a wheel.

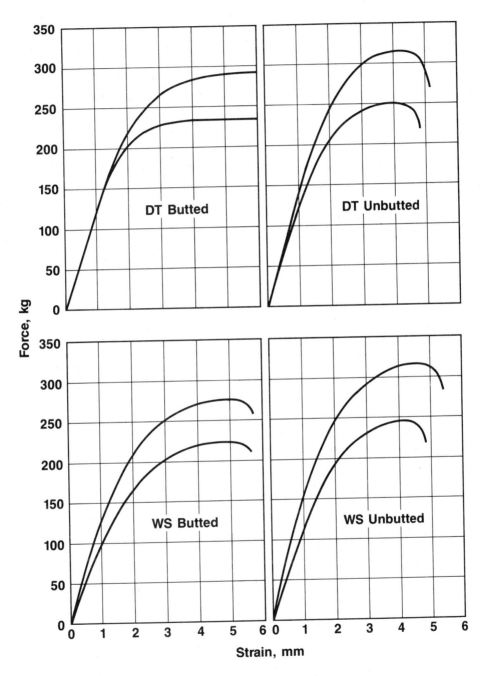

Fig. 69 Spoke strength

EQUATIONS

Various structural formulas were used to determine the values that appear in the text. Some of these equations are shown here. The computation of the wheel deflections for various load combinations is based on a finite element method that divides the wheel into a series of simple structural parts which, with the aid of a computer, can be evaluated through simultaneous solution to a network of equations. However, some of the equations are more practical and are shown here.

SPOKE LENGTHS

To compute spoke lengths the effective rim diameter must be determined to within one millimeter. This is the diameter to which the ends of the fully tensioned spokes extend. Note that a spoke under full tension stretches about one millimeter (as shown in the graphs). The rim, depending on its strength, can also shrink in diameter as much as two millimeters. Determine the flange diameter from center to center of the spoke holes. Determine the width of the flange spacing from center to center of the flanges. Measure the diameter of the spoke hole. Select the spoke crossing pattern and the number of spokes to evaluate the spoke length equation.

1. SPOKE LENGTH

$L = \sqrt{A^2 + B^2 + C^2} - s$ Spoke length (mm)
$A = r \times \sin(T)$ Spoke position offset
$B = R - (r \times \cos(T))$ Radial component
$C = W/2$ Hub half-width
$D = 618mm$ Effective rim diameter
$d = 39mm$ Effective hub diameter
$W = 71mm$ Flange spacing center to center
$w = W/2$ Flange spacing from center
$S = 2.4mm$ Spoke hole diameter
$s = S/2$ Hole radius
$r = d/2$ Hub radius
$R = D/2$ Rim radius
$X = 3$ Cross pattern
$N = 36$ Number of spokes
$T = 720 \times X/N$ Spoke angle

$s = 2.4/2 = 1.2mm$
$R = 618/2 = 309mm$
$r = 39/2 = 19.5mm$
$T = 720 \times 3/36 = 60deg$
$A = 19.5 \times 0.866 = 16.89mm$
$B = 309 - (19.5 \times 0.5) = 299.25mm$
$C = 71/2 = 35.5mm$

$$L = \sqrt{16.89^2 + 299.25^2 + 35.5^2} - 1.2$$

$$L = 300.6mm$$

2. TORSIONAL ELASTICITY OF SPOKING

Elasticity for a typical butted spoke 300mm long

K	$= A \times E/L$	Elasticity (kg/mm)
E	$= 21000$kg/mm²	Modulus of elasticity of steel
L	$= 162$mm	Effective length of spoke
d	$= 1.6$mm	Diameter of spoke shaft
r	$= d/2$	Radius of spoke shaft
A	$= pi \times r^2$	Cross sectional area
r	$= 1.6/2 = 0.8$mm	
A	$= pi \times 0.8^2 = 2.01$mm²	
K	$= 2.01 \times 21000/290 = 145.6$kg/mm	

3. SPOKE ELONGATION FROM TENSION

dL	$= P/K$	Elongation (mm)
K	$= 45.6$kg/mm	Spoke elasticity (from Eq. 2)
P	$= 180$kg	Tension in spoke
dL	$= 180/145.6 = 1.24$mm	

4. TORSIONAL STIFFNESS OF TANGENTIAL SPOKING

Kt	$= dL \times N \times K \times r$	Torsional stiffness (mkg/deg) of hub rotation
K	$= 145.6$kg/mm	Spoke elasticity (from Eq. 2)
N	$= 18$	Number of spokes per flange
r	$= 21$mm	Effective flange radius
dL	$= r \times pi/180$	Spoke elongation per degree of hub rotation

dL $= 21 \times pi/180 = 0.366$mm/deg
Kt $= .366 \times 18 \times 145.6 \times 21$
Kt $= 20143$mmkg/deg
Kt $= 20.1$mkg/deg

5. TORSIONAL STIFFNESS OF A TYPICAL HUB SHAFT

$Kt = K \times G/L$	Torsional stiffness (mkg/deg)
$G = 2640 kg/mm^2$	Shear modulus of aluminum
$r1 = 5.2mm$	Inside radius of shaft
$r2 = 7.3mm$	Outside radius of shaft
$L = 44mm$	Length of shaft
$K = pi \times (r2^4 - r1^4)/2$	Area moment of inertia (mm^4)
$(pi/180)$	Degrees per radian

$$K = pi \times (7.3^4 - 5.2^4)/2 = 3312mm^4$$

$$Kt = 3312 + 2640/44 = 198720 mmkg/rad$$
$$Kt = 198720 \times pi/180/1000 = 3.47 mkg/deg$$

6. TORQUE TRANSFER TO LEFT SIDE OF HUB

$Kt = Ktl + Kts$	Torque stiffness of complete assembly
$Kth = 3.47$ mkg/deg	Torque stiffness of hub shaft
$Kts = 21.4$ mkg/deg	Torque stiffness of spokes (one side)
Ktl	Torque stiffness of hub and left side

Reciprocal relation of parallel parts

$$\frac{1}{Ktl} = \frac{1}{Kth} + \frac{1}{Kts}$$

$$\frac{1}{Ktl} = \frac{1}{3.47} + \frac{1}{21.4} = \frac{1}{3.0}$$

Ktl 3.0
$Kt = 21.4 + 3.0$
$Kt = 24.4 mkg/deg$
Percentage of total stiffness.
On left side $= 100 \times 3.0/24.4$
$\qquad\qquad = 12\%$

7. RIM COMPRESSION FROM SPOKE TENSION

$C = N \times T/(2 \times pi)$ Compression at rim joint (kg)
$N = 36$ Number of spokes
$T = 90kg$ Tension in each spoke

$C = 36 \times 90/(2 \times pi) = 515.6kg$

8. CONSTRICTING FORCE OF INFLATED TIRE ON THE WHEEL

$T = C-E$ Tire tension from inflation (kg)
$P = 8kg/cm^2$ Tire pressure
$d = 2.5 cm$ Diameter of tire cross section
$r = d/2$ Radius of tire cross section
$a = 45deg$ Cord angle in degrees (45 typical)
$A = pi \times r^2$ Cross sectional area of tire
$C = P \times A \times 2 \times tan^2(a)$ Constricting component
$E = P \times A$ Expanding component

$A = pi \times 1.25^2 = 4.91cm^2$

$C = 8 \times 4.91 \times 2 \times 1 = 78.54kg$
$E = 8 \times 4.91 = 39.27kg$
$T = 78.54-39,27 = 39.27kg$
For $T = 0$ the cord angle must be 35.27deg

FINITE ELEMENT COMPUTER ANALYSIS

The wheel deflections plots in figures 8, 9, 10, 12 and 13 were computed by the finite element method. This technique is commonly used for structural analysis of aircraft, bridges, ships, automobiles, and even such things as watch springs. Because the bicycle wheel has identical repetitive elements symmetrically arranged, it allows the use of a simplified method specifically designed for circular structures. For this analysis, the wheel was modeled as a two-dimensional structure. Although the the wheel has three dimensions, nearly all its dynamics are two dimensional, making this model accurate for the values calculated.

The term finite is used in contrast to the essentially infinite complexity of a large structure that can deform simultaneously in varying amounts at different places. The finite element method divides a structure into small, simple, structural sections whose individual deflections can be solved easily. Thus the rim (in a 36-spoke wheel) is divided into 36 short structural beams that reach from spoke to spoke. Each endpoint is called a node.

Each spoke is a single element giving a 36-spoke wheel a total of 72 elements and 37 nodes. Each of these elements is easily defined in structural terms. The rim elements have a resistance to bending, tension and compression, while the spokes resist only tension. Equations are written for each of these conditions based on the material properties and the shape and size of the element. The equations are solved simultaneously to determine the displacement of each node when a specified load is applied at a specific node. The central node at the hub is fixed and, therefore, is not computed.

The 36 active nodes at the rim and spoke junctions are given three degrees of freedom. They can move tangentially, radially, and rotationally in the plane of the wheel. These displacements are computed for each node. This model can be used for both radial and tangential spoking to give results that are as accurate as the measurements used for the rim cross section and spoke dimensions.

To analyze tangential spoking (required for torque loads) the spokes each have a separate node at a distance from the the hub center. The spokes enter the rim at an angle determined by the spoke pattern and hub size. Since the hub nodes of a tangential wheel and the central node of a radial wheel are both fixed in space, they are eliminated from the computation. Angled spokes, however, impart tangential forces to the rim. The torque is introduced by a tangential force at the ground contact point that rotationally displaces the rim with respect to the fixed, central hub.

By using a modified Potters method to solve simultaneous matrix equations, the element sub-matrices are recursively solved until all coefficients for the equation of the wheel have been found. The deflections of each node are related to deflections of each higher numbered node. The deflections of the first node are also related to the deflections of the next higher node at each recursive step. This process provides all the data required to solve the deflection equations for the last node. The value for the last node is then substituted back into the recursive equations until all nodal deflections are found. This method requires about one tenth the computer storage that conventional equation solvers require and it is much faster.

The computed results and the input values from which the deformed wheel graphs were plotted are shown in figures 67 through 71.

```
N SPOKES=      36.00
RADIUS   =     300.00
E SPOKE  =   21000.00
A SPOKE  =       2.00
E RIM    =    7000.00
A RIM    =      77.00
I RIM    =    1124.00
LOAD     =      50.00
LOCATION=      19.00
SPK ANGL=       5.00
```

SPOKE	RADIAL MM	TANGENTIAL MM	ROTATIONAL RADIANS
1	.0069444	-.0206513	-.0000528
2	.0062654	-.0223400	-.0000794
3	.0065904	-.0239973	-.0001001
4	.0074596	-.0257494	-.0000818
5	.0071764	-.0275593	-.0000707
6	.0062864	-.0292832	-.0001045
7	.0067168	-.0309675	-.0001291
8	.0078336	-.0327785	-.0001039
9	.0074715	-.0346630	-.0000888
10	.0063110	-.0364320	-.0001284
11	.0066926	-.0381343	-.0001550
12	.0079012	-.0399681	-.0001260
13	.0078908	-.0419141	-.0001288
14	.0087002	-.0439475	-.0002213
15	.0132743	-.0464587	-.0002637
16	.0141669	-.0494407	.0000079
17	-.0115478	-.0502988	.0007718
18	-.0844696	-.0425248	.0016053
19	-.1531575	-.0219948	-.0000421
20	-.0862531	-.0014889	-.0017748
21	-.0139589	.0066727	-.0009014
22	.0120199	.0062881	-.0001489
23	.0129319	.0035698	.0000837
24	.0088847	.0011671	.0000694
25	.0066331	-.0006882	.0000212
26	.0061078	-.0023162	-.0000078
27	.0063133	-.0039151	-.0000209
28	.0066494	-.0055489	-.0000202
29	.0066294	-.0072136	-.0000182
30	.0063642	-.0088680	-.0000308
31	.0064936	-.0105086	-.0000442
32	.0068966	-.0121837	-.0000392
33	.0067581	-.0138866	-.0000352
34	.0062869	-.0155514	-.0000549
35	.0065158	-.0171937	-.0000719
36	.0071524	-.0189010	-.0000603

Fig. 70 Radial load (see fig. 8)

```
N SPOKES=      36.00
RADIUS  =     300.00
E SPOKE =   21000.00
A SPOKE =       2.00
E RIM   =    7000.00
A RIM   =      77.00
I RIM   =    1124.00
BRAKE F =      50.00
LOCATION=       1.00
SPK ANGL=       5.00
```

SPOKE	RADIAL MM	TANGENTIAL MM	ROTATIONAL RADIANS
1	.0098006	-1.0650647	-.0023095
2	-.0449960	-1.0593797	-.0034538
3	-.0418721	-1.0493209	-.0042344
4	-.0074662	-1.0428415	-.0033165
5	-.0158621	-1.0387350	-.0027382
6	-.0467598	-1.0312000	-.0036925
7	-.0334627	-1.0222941	-.0042112
8	.0012791	-1.0178577	-.0032149
9	-.0083772	-1.0157119	-.0026526
10	-.0393307	-1.0100369	-.0036172
11	-.0260791	-1.0029765	-.0041366
12	.0080895	-1.0003126	-.0031523
13	-.0020555	-.9998490	-.0025925
14	-.0339008	-.9957490	-.0035353
15	-.0223025	-.9900329	-.0040701
16	.0142790	-.9887610	-.0032753
17	.0225737	-.9914943	-.0031543
18	.0304156	-.9957298	-.0043520
19	.0220088	-1.0002859	-.0027908
20	.0118245	-1.0031860	-.0034196
21	.0175049	-1.0058433	-.0029006
22	-.0090018	-1.0067843	-.0032240
23	-.0098914	-1.0054043	-.0040196
24	.0234907	-1.0070764	-.0033875
25	.0216938	-1.0116228	-.0027097
26	-.0090483	-1.0134150	-.0034956
27	-.0008150	-1.0133601	-.0041335
28	.0337585	-1.0172426	-.0033027
29	.0273492	-1.0237029	-.0026990
30	-.0041842	-1.0269476	-.0036065
31	.0067597	-1.0285244	-.0042223
32	.0422585	-1.0343439	-.0033241
33	.0347761	-1.0427334	-.0027528
34	.0036529	-1.0478661	-.0037242
35	.0148434	-1.0513976	-.0042458
36	.0411595	-1.0583832	-.0030517

Fig. 71 Braking load (see fig. 9)

```
N SPOKES=      36.00
RADIUS  =     300.00
E SPOKE =   21000.00
A SPOKE =       2.00
E RIM   =    7000.00
A RIM   =      77.00
I RIM   =    1124.00
LOAD    =      50.00
LOCATION=      19.00
BRAKE F =      50.00
LOCATION=       1.00
SPK ANGL=       5.00
```

SPOKE	RADIAL MM	TANGENTIAL MM	ROTATIONAL RADIANS
1	.0167450	-1.0857160	-.0023623
2	-.0387306	-1.0817197	-.0035332
3	-.0352817	-1.0733183	-.0043345
4	-.0000066	-1.0685909	-.0033983
5	-.0086856	-1.0662942	-.0028089
6	-.0404734	-1.0604832	-.0037970
7	-.0267460	-1.0532616	-.0043403
8	.0091128	-1.0506362	-.0033188
9	-.0009057	-1.0503749	-.0027414
10	-.0330197	-1.0464689	-.0037456
11	-.0193865	-1.0411108	-.0042916
12	.0159908	-1.0402807	-.0032783
13	.0058354	-1.0417631	-.0027212
14	-.0252005	-1.0396965	-.0037566
15	-.0090282	-1.0364915	-.0043339
16	.0284459	-1.0382017	-.0032674
17	.0110259	-1.0417930	-.0023825
18	-.0540540	-1.0382545	-.0027468
19	-.1311487	-1.0222807	-.0028330
20	-.0744286	-1.0046749	-.0051945
21	.0035460	-.9991706	-.0038020
22	.0030181	-1.0004962	-.0033729
23	.0030404	-1.0018345	-.0039360
24	.0323753	-1.0059093	-.0033181
25	.0283269	-1.0123110	-.0026885
26	-.0029405	-1.0157312	-.0035035
27	.0054983	-1.0172752	-.0041544
28	.0404079	-1.0227914	-.0033229
29	.0339786	-1.0309165	-.0027172
30	.0021800	-1.0358156	-.0036373
31	.0132533	-1.0390330	-.0042665
32	.0491552	-1.0465276	-.0033633
33	.0415342	-1.0566200	-.0027880
34	.0099399	-1.0634175	-.0037791
35	.0213593	-1.0685914	-.0043177
36	.0483119	-1.0772842	-.0031120

Fig. 72   Radial and braking load (see fig. 10)

```
N SPOKES=      36.00
RADIUS  =     300.00
E SPOKE =   21000.00
A SPOKE =       2.00
E RIM   =    7000.00
A RIM   =      77.00
I RIM   =    1124.00
SPK ANGL=       5.00
TORQUE  =      50.00
```

SPOKE	RADIAL MM	TANGENTIAL MM	ROTATIONAL RADIANS
1	.0087626	-.9956295	-.0026055
2	-.0217474	-.9943391	-.0035408
3	-.0093931	-.9916075	-.0040843
4	.0245102	-.9931316	-.0031475
5	.0153255	-.9969249	-.0026027
6	-.0152500	-.9973146	-.0035623
7	-.0023768	-.9963018	-.0041090
8	.0317215	-.9995930	-.0031591
9	.0220855	-1.0051357	-.0026200
10	-.0087299	-1.0072289	-.0036064
11	.0046899	-1.0079458	-.0041622
12	.0391995	-1.0130377	-.0031920
13	.0286738	-1.0203454	-.0026399
14	-.0038828	-1.0239887	-.0036420
15	.0089644	-1.0260496	-.0042443
16	.0482376	-1.0328391	-.0034381
17	.0558132	-1.0438321	-.0032395
18	.0544489	-1.0555421	-.0042961
19	.0233154	-1.0647839	-.0024932
20	-.0097507	-1.0634757	-.0033050
21	-.0134871	-1.0591241	-.0029758
22	-.0424457	-1.0519712	-.0033822
23	-.0425049	-1.0423618	-.0041825
24	-.0073844	-1.0361056	-.0034926
25	-.0088419	-1.0329001	-.0027732
26	-.0400241	-1.0268668	-.0035421
27	-.0319285	-1.0189492	-.0041500
28	.0025831	-1.0150193	-.0032945
29	-.0036049	-1.0136674	-.0026789
30	-.0345663	-1.0091018	-.0035457
31	-.0239987	-1.0028979	-.0041106
32	.0101846	-1.0008506	-.0032074
33	.0024173	-1.0012148	-.0026294
34	-.0282344	-.9982658	-.0035376
35	-.0165582	-.9938044	-.0040857
36	.0173786	-.9935578	-.0031621

Fig. 73   Torque load (see fig. 12)

```
N SPOKES=      36.00
RADIUS   =     300.00
E SPOKE  =   21000.00
A SPOKE  =       2.00
E RIM    =    7000.00
A RIM    =      77.00
I RIM    =    1124.00
LOAD     =      50.00
LOCATION=      19.00
SPK ANGL=       5.00
TORQUE   =      50.00
```

SPOKE	RADIAL MM	TANGENTIAL MM	ROTATIONAL RADIANS
1	.0157070	-1.0162808	-.0026583
2	-.0154820	-1.0166790	-.0036201
3	-.0028027	-1.0156049	-.0041844
4	.0319698	-1.0188810	-.0032292
5	.0225019	-1.0244842	-.0026734
6	-.0089636	-1.0265978	-.0036668
7	.0043400	-1.0272694	-.0042381
8	.0395552	-1.0323715	-.0032630
9	.0295571	-1.0397986	-.0027088
10	-.0024189	-1.0436609	-.0037348
11	.0113826	-1.0460801	-.0043172
12	.0471007	-1.0530058	-.0033180
13	.0365646	-1.0622595	-.0027687
14	.0048174	-1.0679362	·-.0038633
15	.0222387	-1.0725083	-.0045080
16	.0624045	-1.0822798	-.0034302
17	.0442654	-1.0941308	-.0024678
18	-.0300207	-1.0980669	-.0026908
19	-.1298422	-1.0867787	-.0025354
20	-.0960038	-1.0649646	-.0050798
21	-.0274461	-1.0524514	-.0038772
22	-.0304258	-1.0456831	-.0035311
23	-.0295730	-1.0387920	-.0040989
24	.0015003	-1.0349386	-.0034231
25	-.0022088	-1.0335883	-.0027520
26	-.0339163	-1.0291830	-.0035499
27	-.0256152	-1.0228642	-.0041709
28	.0092324	-1.0205682	-.0033146
29	.0030245	-1.0208810	-.0026971
30	-.0282021	-1.0179698	-.0035765
31	-.0175051	-1.0134066	-.0041548
32	.0170812	-1.0130343	-.0032465
33	.0091754	-1.0151014	-.0026646
34	-.0219475	-1.0138171	-.0035925
35	-.0100424	-1.0109982	-.0041577
36	.0245310	-1.0124588	-.0032225

Fig. 74 Radial and torque load (see fig. 13)

GLOSSARY

These words are defined with respect to their use in this book, which is not always the same as the principal dictionary use.

alloy	mixture of a pure metal such as iron and a small amount of another metal or metals
buckling	bowing of a column in compression, such as a pole vaulter's pole
butted spoke	spoke which is thicker at the ends than at mid length
compression	pushing force; a chair leg is in compression
conventional tire	a tire with a separate tube and casing; a clincher
deflection	change in shape resulting from a force
deformation	temporary or permanent deflection

derailleur	mechanism which moves a bicycle chain from one sprocket to another
dished wheel	wheel whose rim is not centered over its hub flanges
dynamic	changing, variable, moving
elastic	deforms with complete rebound
elastic limit	boundary between elastic and plastic deformation
elasticity	amount of deformation per unit of force
fatigue	structural weakness resulting from repeated deformation
flange diameter	diameter on which the spoke holes lie in the flange
force	push, pull, twist
freewheel	a mechanism which rotates freely on a shaft in one direction only
gear cluster	several sprockets mounted on a freewheel
high-wheeled bicycle	antique bicycle with one very large front wheel
hub diameter	diameter on which the spoke holes lie in the flanges
hub shaft	thin center part of hub between flanges
inbound spoke	spoke which projects into the hub on insertion
interlacing	placing outbound under inbound spokes at their outer crossing
kilogram (kg)	metric unit of mass (used as a unit of force here) 2.2 pounds
lateral	sideways
load-affected zone	portion of rim which deflects from a load
metal	structural material, iron, steel, aluminum, brass
meter (m)	metric unit of length; meter = 39.37 inches
millimeter (mm)	metric unit of length; 1/1000 meter = 1/25.4 inch
nipple	slender, elongated nut into which spokes thread
outbound spoke	spoke which projects out of the hub on insertion

plastic	deforms without rebound; butter, for instance
pulling spoke	spoke which becomes tighter when the wheel is driven
pushing spoke	spoke which becomes looser when the wheel is driven
radial	extending from a common center
rim compression	force in a wheel rim from the inward force of the spokes
sprocket	toothed wheel to engage a chain
static	fixed, unchanging, constant
stiffness	amount of force per unit of deformation
strain	unit elongation, (mm/mm)
stress	force per unit cross-section area (kg/mm2)
tangent	in contact with the edge of a circle
tangential	in a tangent manner
tension	pulling force; a guitar string is in tension
tensiometer	gauge for measuring tension in wires or spokes
torque	twisting force, a screwdriver transmits torque
torsion	condition resulting from a torque load
true wheel	wheel whose rim appears to stand still when rotated
truing	adjusting spoke tension to make a true wheel
tubular tire	tube-shaped tire containing an integral inner tube; sew-up
unbutted spoke	spoke which is uniformly thick over its entire length
wind drag	force resulting from a body moving through air
wind-up	rotation of the hub of a wheel with respect to the rim
yield point	elastic limit, beginning of plastic

ABOUT THE AUTHOR

Jobst Brandt is well known in the cycling community both as a technical expert and as a rider. He has taught many cyclists how to maintain their bicycles and build wheels in a style that emphasizes demystifying the bicycle and the sport of cycling.

Jobst has ridden competitively, commutes by bicycle, and tours both on and off road in a style that is demanding on equipment and rider.

He is an engineering graduate of Stanford University, worked as a design engineer for Porsche in Germany, and is currently employed at Hewlett-Packard as a research engineer. He is also a design consultant for Avocet Inc.